Beautiful Horses and Ponies

Beautiful Horses and Ponies

Neil Dougall

Produced exclusively for
W H Smith & Son Ltd

Joanne L Mallion

Contents

Special photography for the final chapter was taken at Crabbet Park Equitation, by kind permission of Mr Brian Young.

First published 1976 by Cathay Books Limited 59 Grosvenor Street, London W15 for W. H. Smith & Son Ltd.

ISBN 0 904644 15 4

© 1976 Octopus Books Limited

Produced by Mandarin Publishers Limited 22A Westlands Road, Quarry Bay, Hong Kong

Printed in Hong Kong

The Horse in Europe

The British Isles

The English Thoroughbred is, without doubt, the premier breed of horse in the world, and, as a result, also the most international breed. It was created from a blending at the beginning of the eighteenth century of imported Arabian, Turkoman and Barb blood with the English racing galloway or 'hobby horse', which was described by a writer of the time as being 'bred out of all horses of all nations'.

Three imported stallions—one Arabian, one Turk and one Barb—played decisive roles in building the new breed of racing horse, and every Thoroughbred in the world today is descended in direct male line from one of them. These 'founding fathers' of the magnificent Thoroughbred breed were the Darley Arabian, the Byerley Turk and the Godolphin Barb.

However, the Thoroughbred, while specifically created for racing, has garnered laurels in many other widely differing spheres of activity. In the British Isles its blood has played a major part in producing quality hunters and top-class showjumpers and eventers, as well as elegant hacks, speedy agile polo ponies, and that other latter-day characteristically British creation, the sleek riding pony.

In the United States the most sought-after mount of all, the fast and stocky Quarter Horse, owes much of its popularity to its Thoroughbred blood, while the specialized racing Quarter Horses often have been sired by muscular Quarter Horse-type Thoroughbreds.

In Australia the Thoroughbred is a highly popular sire of stockhorses, the deep-chested long-riding mounts used by Aussie 'ringers' (cowboys) to work beef cattle in the vast Outback. The great majority of 'station sires' are well-conformed retired racehorses from one of the big coastal cities, and they roam with their bands of hardy broodmares over many thousands of acres of bushland.

Australia's renowned Waler, whose descendants are known as Australian Stockhorses, carried much Thoroughbred blood, and when India belonged to Britain, Walers were much in demand as remounts and artillery horses.

In Europe the Thoroughbred has been much used for crossing with other breeds, but nowhere to greater effect than in France, which produces exceptional Anglo-Arabs—crosses of Thoroughbred and Arab—which are outstanding general-purpose riding horses. And in Spain there is the Hispano-Anglo-Arabe, the Andalusian-Thoroughbred-Arab blend, which is fast, agile, bold yet even-tempered, and much in demand for working the fierce fighting bulls.

The key to the Thoroughbred's world-wide pre-eminence both as racer and riding horse is its unique combination of great speed, long, free, easy action, unequalled courage, superb quality and magnificently balanced conformation.

In the British Isles the great majority of quality hunters are sired by Thoroughbreds. The hunter is not a breed but a *type* of horse, the one that will best carry riders of various weights safely, comfortably and relatively quickly over the countryside while hunting fox or stag. This is a general definition —when it comes to specifics, the suitability of a hunter for its job will also depend to a very large degree on the type of country over which it is to be ridden. In the Shires, that part of the Midlands which is regarded as the best English hunting country, the type of hunter which will fare best in

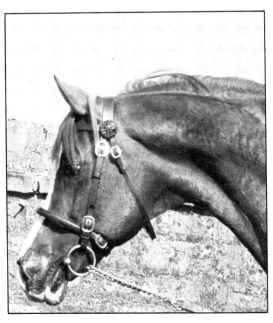

A well-conformed
Thoroughbred stallion:
the Thoroughbred is the
premier breed of horse
in the world and the
most international
Far left: El Meluk, an
Arab stallion, has been
a British National
Champion. He is by
Mikeno (left),
another champion; both
horses display the
characteristic Arabian
dished face

the big, well-fenced pastures will be Thoroughbred or very close to it. Yet such a mount might well be out of place in areas of small enclosures and big woodlands, in ploughland or in rough, hilly areas. In this sort of country a short-legged compact horse with a very equable temperament is often best, and would probably have been produced by crossing a Thoroughbred with one of Britain's native breeds, such as the Connemara, Highland or Welsh Cob.

Ireland is famous for its hunters, and the classic breeding formula is to cross Thoroughbred stallions with Irish Draught mares. The superb results are big horses with lots of bone that can really stride on and leap, and carry a heavy weight all day.

The type at which breeders of hunters should aim is epitomized by the show hunter, which, in fact, because of his high value, may never actually go hunting! Still, the show hunter is there as an ideal on which hunter breeders should set their sights. The horse must be well proportioned, with strong back, loins and quarters, have a well-sloped

shoulder and, overall, give a distinct impression of substance and power. A deep girth, with plenty of heart room is essential, and so are really good sound, strong limbs.

As well as looking good, though, the show hunter must also be able to move extremely well, with a long, low, effortless gallop, as well as a free and straight walk and trot. The judges of show hunters also look for equable temperament, good manners and a good mouth.

Then there are working hunters, which are judged at shows on the basis of 40 per cent for jumping ability, 30 per cent for conformation and 30 per cent for ride and action. The course that the working hunters jump consists of six natural-looking obstacles of various types, and the accent in judging is most definitely on the style the working hunter shows as he negotiates the fences. Travelling smoothly at a good hunting pace, he is expected to display calm, free jumping.

Another famous type of riding horse in Britain

Hackney, which many claim to be the finest harness horse in the world. To see a really good Hackney in action in the show ring, with its proud fiery presence and its extremely high, elegant action, is to remember it forever. Such horses truly seem to float over the close-cut turf.

If one looks attentively at the Hackney's impressive action, one sees that the shoulder moves freely and progressively, with a high, ground covering knee action, the foreleg being thrown well forward and not just picked up and down. The action of the hind legs is, to a lesser degree, the same, and it is straight and true, with no hint of 'dishing' or 'plaiting'. Standing still, the good Hackney is also impressive: head held high with ears pricked, forelegs straight and firmly planted, and hindlegs placed back so that the animal covers the maximum of ground.

The Cleveland Bay is an ancient British breed which comes from the north of England. It started out, with its endurance and weight-carrying capacity, as an all-purpose animal, and was particularly in demand as a packhorse. The Cleveland Bay was also ridden across the rough country of its Yorkshire homeland, was used on farms and to follow hounds, and later became the most popular carriage horse.

In appearance, the Cleveland Bay is usually a bright bay with black points, and stands 15·2 to 16 hands high. It has a large, well-made body, with a relatively long back and fairly low withers. Its head is fairly large and its neck is long. The Cleveland's legs are short, hard and clean cut.

Arabian
riding h
parts of
their sta
them pa
suited t
riding

Britain's heavy horses—the Clydesdale, the Shire and the Suffolk Punch—have a stirring history. They all stem from the big powerful horses which were used as mounts in battle by the heavily-armoured knights of the Middle Ages. When, with the invention of gunpowder, their role in battle came to an end, the heavy horses found other arduous, if considerably less glorious, fields of endeavour on the farm and in transport work.

The Clydesdale comes from the Clyde valley, an area which has always been regarded as the best horse-breeding country in Scotland. Most of the horses used to carry Scottish knights were bred there, and, after King Edward I of England imposed a ban on the export of military horses to Scotland, breeding stock was imported from Flanders and Denmark. Finally, the so-called 'gig' mares of the area were crossed with stallions from Flanders in the latter part of the eighteenth century to give rise to the modern Clydesdale.

The origins of the Shire horse, a tall, imposing, tremendously powerful animal with a wide chest, can be traced back to Tudor times. As its name implies, it originated in the Shires (in particular, the counties of Staffordshire, Derbyshire and Leicestershire), and the breed was founded with mares from the stock of the Old English Black Horse, which was bred on the east coast to the north of East Anglia. The truly impressive Shire is famed for its strength, stamina and robust constitution.

The Suffolk Punch is also strong, hardy and docile, as well as remarkably long-lived. It is not as tall as the Shire, which can stand as high as 18 hands, but it weighs just as much, with a deep, round-ribbed barrel and short, very strong cannon bones. The breed originated in Suffolk, but has long been considered native to the whole area of East Anglia. It seems that the foundation stock of the breed may have been brought to Britain by the Vikings, since the Suffolk Punch is very similar in many respects to the Jutland horse from the other side of the North Sea. Suffolk Punches are always chesnut in colour, although there are seven acknowledged shades, varying from a dark to a bright chesnut.

France

The great bulk of horse-breeding in France takes place under government control, this guidance being exerted through the National Stud Administration of the Ministry of Agriculture. The National Stud Administration keeps the various stud books, including that of the Thoroughbred, and also makes its stallions available to breeders at very low fees. National stud farms dot the countryside, some of the best known being Haras du Pin in Normandy, Haras de Pompadour, with its

imposing chateau, in the Limousin, and Tarbes, in Gascony, where, once a year, a whole week is dedicated to the exhibiting, buying and selling of the world-renowned French Anglo-Arab.

France also has a large private Thoroughbred breeding industry, with most of the stud farms concentrated in the Normandy area. Thoroughbreds were first taken to France from England towards the end of the eighteenth century, and in 1833 the *Société d'Encouragement*, which still oversees French racing, was founded. By the middle of the nineteenth century the French clearly demonstrated that they had 'arrived' on the Thoroughbred breeding scene—in 1865 French-bred Gladiateur won England's Triple Crown (Two Thousand Guineas, Derby and St Leger) and the Grand Prix de Paris as a three-year-old, and at four he won the Ascot Gold Cup and two leading French distance races. His statue stands today just inside the entrance gates of Longchamp racecourse in Paris.

Horses other than Thoroughbreds also race in France, however. They are designated A.Q.P.S. (*Autre que pur sang*) and compete in steeplechases, including France's characteristic cross-country steeplechase in which the horses race across open country along a course marked out with flags and jump true cross-country obstacles.

Trotting races are extremely popular in France, with events for trotters pulling gigs and also

for ridden trotters. Trotters were first bred in France in the eighteenth century, but racing them did not start until 1836, at a track at Cherbourg. The foundation blood for the French Trotter came from the Norman horse—two imported English hunter stallions covered Norman mares whose offspring then proved to be exceptionally fast trotters. Careful breeding and the judicious addition of

Below : the first French-bred Thoroughbred to achieve international renown, Gladiateur won the English Triple Crown of Two Thousand Guineas, Derby and St. Leger in 1865

Thoroughbred blood eventually resulted in a clearly defined trotting breed, which was recognized at the beginning of this century. Today's most valued harness race for trotters is the internationally famous Prix d'Amerique, for four-year-olds and over, and the most prestigious event for ridden trotters is the Prix du Président de la République, for four-year-olds.

The justly famed French Anglo-Arab is used for racing (in particular, steeplechasing), show-jumping, hunting, eventing, dressage and general pleasure riding. This breed stems from two formerly separate sources—the Demi-Sang Anglo-Arabe (part-bred Anglo-Arab), which was also known as the Southern part-bred or the Tarbes horse; and the Pur-Sang Anglo-Arabe (pure-bred Anglo-Arab), which descends from a direct cross of Thoroughbred with pure-bred Arabian. The Southern part-bred resulted from using Thoroughbreds or pure-bred Arabians on mares carrying much Arabian blood, and whose bloodlines were documented.

Anglo-Arabs in France have their own stud book, which they share with pure-bred Arabians, and to be eligible a minimum of 25 per cent Arab blood is required. Both sire and dam must have been registered in the stud book as Anglo-Arabs or Arabs, or, if one of them is Thoroughbred, in the stud book for Thoroughbreds.

Interestingly enough, there is not much breeding of pure-bred Arabians in France, and the score or so of Arabian stallions in the country are mainly used for the production of Anglo-Arabs, either covering Thoroughbred mares for the direct first cross, or Anglo-Arab mares whose owners want to increase the Arabian blood in the progeny. Before and after World War II nearly all the Arabian stallions purchased by the National Studs came from the Middle East, but recently they have turned to Poland for imported Arabian sires.

The Selle Français, or French Saddle Horse, is a very recent designation which resulted from a general reorganization of the breeding of part-breds. Several years ago all the various part-breds, such as the Demi-Sang Vendéen, Charollais, Normand, etc., were grouped together under the general name of Selle Français. This useful riding animal is produced mainly by crossing Thoroughbred stallions with part-bred mares, although part-bred and Anglo-Arab stallions are increasingly being used. Only the foal of a pedigreed part-bred mare can be registered in the stud book for the Selle Français, and only a pedigreed mare may be covered by a Thoroughbred stallion.

France also has its share of draught horses, with the main breeds being the Boulonnais, the Ardennais, the Breton and the Percheron. Probably the best known of them all, internationally, is the Percheron, which has quite a lot of Arabian blood.

West Germany

There are three main breeds of warm-blooded horses in West Germany today—the Hanoverian, the East Prussian, or Trakehner, and the Holstein. Thoroughbreds are also bred in West Germany,

14

where there is a burgeoning interest in racing, and a small number of Arabians are produced as well.

Probably the best known of West Germany's horses outside the country is the Hanoverian, which is a good jumper and has showjumped with success at the big international shows. This breed originally came from north-west Germany—from Brunswick, Brandenburg, Mecklenburg and Pomerania. Native mares were crossed with Thoroughbred, Cleveland Bay, Mecklenburg, Norfolk Roadster and East Prussian stallions to produce a variety of strains that found their respective uses as agricultural, coach and artillery horses, as well as saddle horses and even racehorses of a type.

Latterly, however, the emphasis in the breeding of the Hanoverian has shifted towards producing a lighter and more refined saddle horse with a somewhat high action. These sell well, and for

good prices, and at the beginning of this decade almost 7,000 mares were listed in the stud book for Hanoverians.

The East Prussian, or Trakehner, horse is, like so many other inhabitants of West Germany, a refugee from the East. The members of the breed that founded the present flourishing Trakehner population of West Germany at the end of World War II went through one of the most rigorous selective tests that any breed has had to face at any time in history.

This harrowing ordeal began when the advancing Russian armies started to overrun East Prussia, the ancestral home of the breed. With Russian gunfire sounding in their ears and with flames already leaping from the outer-lying farms, the Trakehner breeders harnessed their animals to their carts and wagons, tied others behind, and began an

A Trakehner stallion strikes a dramatic pose for the photographer at the Redefin Stud in East Germany, where horses have been bred for almost 250 years

15

Donauwind, a champion Trakehner stallion; the Trakehner is a native of East Prussia, and is also known as the East Prussian Horse

unprecedented flight to the West through the unrelenting snow and ice of a Central European midwinter. Three months and 900 miles (1450 km) later, what remained of the horses and the families that had bred them were safe—but from a total prewar population of more than 50,000 Trakehners, only 700 mares and a handful of stallions had survived. For weeks on end during the agonising trek to the West, the animals were never unharnessed from the wagons they pulled. The ensuing foaling and breeding season was surely the most bitter on record for any breed at any time—most of the mares either aborted or produced dead foals, and nearly all of them failed to get in foal again that year. But the very best of the tough, game, iron-hard East Prussian horses had overcome appalling odds in fighting their way to the West—and such stock provided the basis of the very impressive and extremely attractive Trakehner breed of today.

Another major achievement of the Trakehner was the use of its blood in the foundation of the Swedish warm-blood breed, which is outstanding as a dressage mount. The Swedish warm-blood is, in fact, based almost wholly upon East Prussian blood.

The Holstein horse is not as popular as it once was, and consequently the breed has been decreasing in numbers. It used to be called the Marsh horse because the breed originated in the marshes of the Elbe River, and in those early days (the seventeenth century) the horses were large and strong, with a high action, and convex heads which were inherited from Neapolitan and Spanish ancestors. Later, Cleveland Bay, Turkoman and Thoroughbred blood was added, and two main strains were developed—one of heavy coach and artillery horses, and the other of middleweight saddle horses. Still later again, both of these strains were mingled to produce a good showjumping horse.

Austria and Hungary

Austria is the home of the famous Lipizzaner of Vienna's Spanish Riding School, the internationally-known 'dancing' white horse which has been the subject of so many books and films, particularly during the last two decades.

The Lipizzaner breed was founded in 1580 when nine Andalusian stallions and 24 Andalusian mares were brought to Lipizza, a small village near Trieste, from Spain. At the time the ancient Andalusian breed was the most sought-after in Europe, and was especially suited for the high-stepping, refined and elegant displays of classical riding that were a feature of every important Court.

At first the breed of transplanted Spanish horses was refreshed from time to time with more imports from the Iberian Peninsula, and later, when the importation of horses from Spain became difficult, recourse was made to other breeds closely related to the original Andalusian. Finally, about 1816, Arabian blood was introduced in the form of the Arabian stallion Siglavy, a horse which founded one of the six main strains of Lipizzaner at the Spanish Riding School today.

The six male strains existent today can be traced to the following founding stallions: Pluto, a grey foaled in 1765 and brought from Denmark, although of direct Spanish descent; Conversano, a black Neapolitan (this breed also derives from Spanish blood) born in 1767; Favory, a dun Kladruber born in 1779; Neapolitano, a bay foaled in Italy in 1790; Siglavy, the grey Arabian mentioned above, born in 1810; and Maestoso, a grey foaled in 1819, of Spanish and Neapolitan blood.

Fourteen of the original female lines still exist among the mares living at the present-day stud farm of the Spanish School Lipizzaners at Piber in Styria.

Nearly all Lipizzaners are white, and breeding to produce pure white horses was begun early in the breed's history. Today, in accordance with the laws of genetics, the odd bay Lipizzaner is foaled, and, while one bay stallion is always kept at the School in Vienna as a matter of tradition, the bays are never bred from.

However, while the classic Lipizzaner is a pure shining white at maturity, it is born dark brown or charcoal grey, and only slowly does its coat acquire the hue for which it is famed. Some young Lipizzaners begin to turn grey, as a prelude to turning white, at three years of age. Others do not start to go grey until they are five or six. However, whether turning grey or still dark, those of the colts which are selected to go to the Spanish Riding School to be trained in their exacting routines are taken from their mountain pastures at the age of three and a half.

For identification purposes, and following traditional custom, the Lipizzaners are branded profusely, and each strain has its own marking. The stud brand, today a 'p' for Piber surmounted by a crown, is put on the left croup. Then the so-called ancestral brand, a symbol of the dam's sire and the initial of one or other of the six stallion lines, is placed on the spot covered by the saddle. On the right side under the saddle goes the number under which the horse is registered, and finally on the left cheek is placed an 'L', standing for Lipizzaner.

Stallions only are ridden at the school, and each of them bears a double-barrelled name derived

Hungarian half-bred colts out at grass at the Dalmand Stud

17

A herd of Lipizzaner mares and foals have a watchful eye kept on them at Szilvasvarad in Hungary
Right: the Mesohegyes Stud, where this photograph was taken, was founded in 1785 by Maria Theresa

from those of the sire and dam, e.g. Neapolitano Africa, Maestoso Alea, etc.

In Austria's neighbour Hungary, which was linked to it so intimately in the Austro-Hungarian Empire, exists what has been from time immemorial a sort of earthly paradise for horses—the vast grassy expanse of the rolling *puszta*. Horses flourished in Hungary from before recorded history and the people of the land were always famed as fine horsemen. At the height of the power of the Austro-Hungarian Empire, Hungary formed the core of the largest organization of government horse-breeding establishments in Europe, and in the latter half of the eighteenth century the Austro-Hungarian state stud at Radautz was the biggest stud complex in all Europe. Situated in the Suczawa River valley were twelve breeding farms and five large pasture estates for Thoroughbred, Arabian and Oriental horses. Another famous large Imperial stud was that of Mesohegyes, established in 1785.

The basic role of these studs was to produce cavalry horses and remounts, which gave rise to a number of uniquely Hungarian breeds, such as the Nonius, Furioso and North Star. Gidran Nonius, the stallion from which this breed takes its name, was brought from France during the first half of the nineteenth century to be crossed with mares of Spanish blood. Later, Siglavy Arabian blood was added to complete the creation of the new breed. Nowadays there are both large and small Nonius, the smaller carrying more Arabian blood.

Furioso, the foundation sire of the breed of that name, was a Thoroughbred foaled in 1836, and the black North Star, the basic progenitor of another Hungarian breed, was also a Thoroughbred.

The Gidran, which today is a rather long-backed chestnut standing about 16 hands high, had as its founder a stallion named Gidran Senior, which was imported from Arabia in 1818. Actually, it was one of his sons, named Gidran II, the dam of which was an Andalusian, which had the most impact on the breed. The Gidran was originally used as a cavalry mount, but today it is popular as a showjumper and also as a carriage horse.

In 1889 the Babolna Stud was added to the Austro-Hungarian government network, with its initial principal aim being that of producing stallions to sire animals for agricultural work. Nowadays, however, the Babolna State Stud is famed for breeding some of the finest Arabians in the world.

Probably the best known of all Hungarian breeds is a type of Arabian, the Shagya. Hungarian Arabs of the Shagya strain are all descended from the Arabian stallion Shagya I, acquired in Syria in 1836. His direct descendants Shagya XXXII and Shagya XXXIX are standing at stud in Hungary today!

Spain and Portugal

Spain's great gift to the world of horses was the Andalusian. For hundreds of years this noble, high-stepping horse with the broad chest and flowing mane and tail was the most desired mount in Europe. In the seventeenth century the Andalusian was described by England's famous high school horseman, the Duke of Newcastle, as '. . . the noblest horse in the world, the most beautiful that can be. He is of great spirit and of great courage and

docile, hath the proudest walk, the proudest trot and the best action in his trot; the loftiest gallop and is the lovingest and gentlest horse and fittest of all for a King in day of Triumph.'

During the glorious years of Spain's Golden Age the Andalusian made much stirring history, both in Europe and the Americas. In Austria in the sixteenth century Andalusians were used, as we have seen above, to lay the firm foundations of the Lipizzaners of the Spanish Riding School of Vienna, and Andalusian blood also exerted its influence on breeds in many other European countries.

Across the Atlantic, Andalusians were the mounts of the Spanish conquistadores, those few mounted men who explored and conquered so much of North, Central and South America for Spain. The role played by the horses was crucial, and Hernan Cortes, who captained a mere handful of riders in the overthrow of the Aztecs and the conquest of Mexico, gratefully proclaimed, 'After God, we owed our victory to the horses!'

In the Americas today, Andalusian blood lives on in many breeds, including the Quarter Horse, the Appaloosa, the Saddle Horse, the Pinto, the Palamino and the Mustang in the United States and Mexico, the Criollo in Argentina, the Peruvian Paso

The elegant Andalusian of Spain has been bred for hundreds of years, and is still much in demand for breeding and riding purposes today

in Peru, the Colombian Paso in Colombia and the Paso Fino in Puerto Rico.

The classic Andalusian is still to be found in Spain, and its popularity has, in fact, been increasing year by year, with animals exported to countries all round the globe. Even Australia, so distant from Spain, now has its own national Andalusian Association!

At first sight the classic Andalusian is very impressive with its sculptural beauty, proud bearing, natural high action and friendly, docile temperament. The Andalusian is strongly built and yet very elegant, naturally high-stepping, but with catlike agility; and while it presents a picture of spirited animation under saddle or led in hand, it is at all times perfectly amenable to the will of the person controlling it.

The Andalusian's beauty is a balanced symmetry of noble proportions that was the model for the great sculptors of Europe for hundreds of years. The head is majestic, with large, kind, well-set eyes, a broad forehead, and well-placed ears. The neck is reasonably long, broad yet elegant, and well-crested in the stallions. Well-defined withers precede a short back (from this comes the Andalusian's great agility) which joins with broad, strong quarters. The croup is gently rounded, the tail is set rather low, and the long mane and tail are luxuriantly silky. The horse's shoulders are long and sloping, the chest is impressively broad, and the barrel is well ribbed out. The legs are of medium length, clean cut and elegant, yet more than strong enough to support the robustness of the body. Most Andalusians average around 15·2 hands high, weigh something over 1,000 pounds (450 kg) and are white, grey or bay in colour. Black and roan Andalusians are also seen, but more rarely.

The temperament of the Andalusian is one of its outstanding features and is truly exceptional—it is one of the most naturally friendly and docile of all breeds, and this calm good nature and ease of handling is a most welcome feature of even serving stallions. Yet, amazingly enough, even though the Andalusian is so docile, it moves with a great deal of spirited animation.

Many Andalusians 'dish' extravagantly, and this showy action is very much in demand among the Cordoban-hatted riders of Spain's far south. High, wide and handsome is how they want their stallions to come prancing down the garlanded streets of Andalusia's white towns during fiesta time, so they seek proud mounts whose knees come flashing right up in front of their broad chests, and whose forelegs rotate showily out to the side as the horses move majestically forward.

The origin of the Andalusian is not definitely known, although most present-day Spanish authorities maintain that it is native to the Iberian Peninsula, and that it does not owe any feature of its make-up to foreign horses. Nevertheless, a fairly convincing theory is that the Moors developed and fixed the Andalusian as a breed during their centuries-long occupation of southern Spain, crossing their desert-bred Barbs with mares they found in the Peninsula to establish this uniquely Spanish breed.

In Spain today the Andalusian is still mainly bred in the sun-baked south, with Jerez de la Frontera, Seville and Cordoba as the main centres. There are less than 2,000 pure-breds in Spain today, and really first-class examples of the breed are very restricted in number.

Right: in spring and early summer, horses and ponies will put on flesh and improve their condition on rich new grass, but should not be allowed to overeat and become fat
Opposite: hunt servants pause by a covert on a crisp winter day. Fox hunting has been a popular sport in England, Ireland and the United States for several centuries

*A beautifully turned out
pair at a ploughing match*

A magnificent prize-winning Shire horse on parade at a show

Right: the Breton horse, one of the best-known French heavy horse breeds, is both docile and strong
Below: herds of Camargue horses still roam this marshy part of Southern France

A superb photograph of
the beautiful and
intricate harness still
worn by brewery horses
in parts of Germany

Above: the Furioso breed, named after its founder stallion, has become popular throughout Eastern Europe
Right: the beautiful Akhal-Teké is a desert horse, bred for thousands of years in Russia, where the purity of the breed is still rigorously guarded
Opposite: an unusual example of teamwork: four Russian Don horses harnessed to a racing tachanka

Above: mares and foals, coats gleaming with health, graze on a stud in Hungary
Right: an example of the curious markings of spotted horses: this is an Austrian Pinzgauer
Opposite above: a Russian Lokai carrying a rider wearing traditional ceremonial Tadjik costume
Opposite below: three robust Don foals

Andalusians are crossed with Arabians and Thoroughbreds to produce excellent general-purpose riding horses. The boldest, fastest and most agile of these are selected for very special work —they are used to work the touchy-tempered, fast and dangerous fighting bulls in their huge dry pastures. When the big black bulls start to play rough, the Andalusian *vaquero* needs a talented mount on which he can literally stake his life; the Thoroughbred and the Arabian provide the speed in the cross-bred, and the Andalusian supplies the bold yet calm temperament, and the turn-on-a-peseta agility.

The Andalusian also makes a spectacular high school mount and is used as such by the gentlemen horseback bullfighters, the *rejoneadores*, when they ride ahead of the glittering parade into the bullring. Sitting his Andalusian stallion in taut arrogance, the *rejoneador* guides the horse through the Spanish Walk and the Spanish Trot, the *passage* and the *piaffe*, the *pirouette* and Half and Full Passes. Often the display of high school will be perfectly climaxed

by one of the truly spectacular soaring leaps.

The Lusitano horse of Portugal is closely related to the Andalusian, but while some strains of Lusitano are of very high quality indeed, in general these horses tend to be longer-backed, longer-legged and bigger-headed than the Andalusian. Often, too, they have very long ears and exaggerated Roman noses.

Another Portuguese horse containing much Andalusian blood, and a very fine horse at that, is the Alter Real. This is a tall, very impressive bay horse with great presence, a natural high action, and a very handsome head and neck. There are very few of these horses, and a really good one is greatly prized.

In both Spain and Portugal there are a number of stud farms breeding Arabians, some of the best stock belonging to the government studs. Spain has considerably more Arabians than Portugal, and most of them come from the southernmost region of Andalusia. The countryside there is reputed to be very similar to the best Arabian-breeding areas of

The Lusitano is a native of Portugal, in many respects similar to Spain's Andalusian. Its agility and obedience stand it in good stead in the bullring
Opposite: a French farmer leads his roan heavy horse along the furrows; genuine workhorses can still be seen in many parts of the world

33

the Middle East, and certainly that part of Spain does produce some marvellous-looking Arabians of desert-type—lean-bodied and stylized, with excellent steel-tendoned limbs and hard feet, and magnificent heads showing the much-sought-after quality of 'dryness'. The best of Spain's Arabians are not only very beautiful to look at, they give the impression of being tough riding horses well up to the task of carrying a rider easily and for a long time over testing terrain.

Poland and Russia

Poland is justly famed for its high-quality Arabians, some of the best of which have been exported to various parts of the world during recent years, where they have done scintillatingly well in showring competitions.

Arabians have been bred in Poland for more than 300 years, with much attention being paid to the preservation of true desert type, soundness, fertility and temperament. An Arabian's soundness or lack thereof is tested in the most practical way possible in Poland—the horses are raced for one or more seasons.

The first exportation of Polish Arabians to a Western country after World War II was made to Britain in 1958. In ensuing years Arabian breeders in more and more countries sought them out, and they have done particularly well in the United States, where the Arabian is very popular and many shows and other competitions are staged especially for them. One famous Polish stallion that achieved outstanding success in America was Bask, which

won the American National Championship in hand, under saddle and in harness on three successive occasions—and whose daughters also did extremely well in the showring at the highest level.

However, Poland has several very good native breeds. There is the Wielkopolski, a half-bred hunter type with East Prussian blood in its background; and the Malopolski, which is a lighter, smaller horse with Arab half-bred and Anglo-Arab origins.

The present-day Wielkopolski is a large, good-looking horse which can be ridden or driven. In its genetic background are several older Polish breeds such as the Poznan and the Masuren.

The Malopolski is said to be the closest in type to the original Polish horse, and owes a lot to the influence of Arabian blood. It is handsome, elegant, sound and agile, with plenty of stamina.

There are, not surprisingly, a large number of different breeds of horses spread across the vast expanse of the USSR. However, four breeds stand out like shining lights—the Turkoman, the Don, the Bujonny and the Orlov Trotter.

The Turkoman, a lean, tough and superbly stylized desert horse, is one of the very oldest breeds on earth—chargers of a very similar type to today's Turkoman were ridden by the bodyguard of King Darius of Persia as long ago as 500 BC. The Turkoman has a golden-coated descendant of fame and great stamina, the Akhal-Teké. One remarkable animal of this breed once covered 2,580 miles (4,150 km), 600 (965 km) of which were across sandy desert, in 84 days! There is much evidence to show that Turkoman blood played a very important part in the shaping of the English Thoroughbred.

Don horses are hard and tough, and are general-purpose animals, being used for riding, pulling carts and for farm work. The breed originated during the eighteenth and nineteenth centuries in the rugged area bordering the Don River, and evolved from a small, fiery Oriental type of horse known as the Old Don which was later crossed with Orlov Trotters and the Orlov-Rostopschin.

The Bujonny was shaped from a cross of the Don and the Thoroughbred, and has produced some excellent jumpers.

The Orlov Trotter, surely one of the most famous of Russian breeds, owes its existence to the genius of a single horse-breeder, Count Orlov-Tschmenski, and to one outstanding and prepotent stallion, Bars I, foaled in 1784.

The Akhal-Teké of Russia is a lean desert horse of superb quality

Count Orlov wished to create a breed of horse that would be tough and strong, able to cover great distances during the hard Russian winter while pulling a sleigh or *troika*. He started off by importing a number of Arabian stallions, one of which, Smetanka, proved to have exceptional trotting ability. He was crossed with a blue-dun Danish mare (which probably was descended from Spanish bloodlines) to produce the stallion Polkan. This horse was not, however, everything that the keen eye of the Count desired, and he was mated in turn with a Dutch Harddraver mare.

The result of this mating was the great Bars I, which was not only an exceptional individual himself, but a tremendously prepotent stallion which 'stamped' his stock with his own so-desirable likeness. He was a long-lived sire, too, standing at stud for all of seventeen years.

The Horse in the Americas

North America

By far the most popular breed in North America is the fast, agile, even-tempered Quarter Horse, the ideal mount of the cowboy. The very muscular but still refined Quarter Horse is the fastest horse in the world over short distances, and this, allied to its superb agility and innate 'cow sense', means that it has no rival when it comes to working cattle on the ranches. It is also much in demand as a rodeo mount, and the fastest Quarter Horses of all, many of which have been sired by Thoroughbreds, take part in special quarter mile races, some of which carry very high prize money.

It was from competing in such races that the Quarter Horse derived its name. In pioneering times in North America there was much interest in horse racing but very few racetracks. Competitions were therefore staged in the main streets of the towns, and few of those streets were more than a quarter of a mile (400 metres) long. Horse owners who wanted to race consequently looked for powerful sprinting animals that could hurl themselves forward from a standstill into a blur of action and maintain great speed until the finish was reached. A bold, keen, yet very equable temperament was also an obvious advantage for a horse of this kind, and fortunately the Spanish background in the Quarter Horse provided just that desirable cast of mind. At the same time, a horse with such attributes was a 'natural' for working cattle, and racing and everyday ranch work have thus been intertwined in the background of the Quarter Horse from very early days.

However, it was only in 1941 that the Quarter Horse was officially recognized as a breed. Since then, this all-American horse has increased in popularity by leaps and bounds so that today it is by far the most numerous of any North American breed, and is exported to many countries.

The Quarter Horse usually stands from 14·3 to 15·1 hands high, and weighs between 1,100 and 1,300 pounds (500 and 590 kg). A good example of the breed should have a short, attractive head with a small muzzle, foxy ears and a well-developed jaw. His neck should be of medium length, meeting the body at an angle of some 45 degrees, and should be neither heavily crested nor too light. Shoulders should be well laid-back to slope at about 45 degrees, and the chest should be fairly wide and deep, with plenty of heart room. The back should be short and powerful, especially across the loins, the barrel should be well ribbed-out and the legs fairly short and packed with muscle. A particular feature of the Quarter Horse's conformation is its hindquarters, which should be very broad and heavily muscled, especially in the thigh and gaskin. In fact, viewed from the rear, the Quarter Horse should be wider from stifle to stifle than through the hips.

It is from this enormously strong and so-characteristic rear end that the Quarter Horse gets the great power it needs for quick starting and for covering a short distance of ground faster than any other horse on earth.

There are two basic types of Quarter Horse —the stocky, very heavily muscled 'bulldog' type, which is the epitome of the working cowhorse, and the more elegant racing type, which usually carries more recent Thoroughbred blood in its pedigree.

The supremely popular Quarter Horses are put to many more uses besides working cattle and racing, however. They are ridden in the various

rodeo and Western contests such as reining, barrel racing, trail horse, pole bending, etc., and they are also used under English-style tack in pleasure, jumping, working hunter and polo pony events.

An especially prized type of Quarter Horse is the Palomino, adding to all its other desirable attributes the lovely golden sheen which Western riders find so appealing.

The Quarter Horse has also played a very important role in setting the basic cowhorse type of several other major American Western breeds, principally the Appaloosa and the Paint.

The Appaloosa is a spotted horse, originally bred by the valiant Nez Percé Indians from Spanish stock. Judicious additions of Quarter Horse blood to this unusually marked breed have made the better individuals top-class Western horses with speed, agility and even temperaments to match their eye-catching coat patterns.

The Paint, or Pinto, is another 'coloured' Western horse which owes much to the Quarter Horse. The American Paint Horse Association, founded in 1962 to upgrade the quality of the breed, insists that any horse which applies for registration must have been sired by an APHA stallion, a registered Quarter Horse or a Thoroughbred.

The ideal conformation of the Paint is very close to that of the Quarter Horse, and there are two basic colour patterns—the Tobiano, a predominantly white horse with large patches of colour, especially on head, flanks and chest, and white often spreading unbroken across the back, and the Overo, a solid-coloured animal with white mainly on the mid-part of the body and rarely spreading across the back. In addition to white, the accepted body colours of the Paint are black, bay, sorrel, dun, palomino and roan.

One very interesting aspect of the Paint is that no two horses ever carry exactly the same markings —they are as individual, in fact, as human beings' fingerprints.

These, then, are the modern horses of the American West, but there is one archetypal Western horse which is still to be found in small herds in the most rugged parts of the West today. This is the legendary Mustang, the original mount of the Indians, and also of the first trappers, hunters and cowboys to wrestle with the once-savage land.

The word 'mustang' is a corruption of the Spanish word *mesteño*, and the Mustang is a direct descendant of Spanish horses taken to North America by the early Spanish explorers and settlers which escaped into the wild. There they multiplied quickly, at the same time degenerating in size and type due to uncontrolled inbreeding and to the rigours of the hard life they lived.

Successfully spanning the worlds of Western and so-called 'English' riding in America is the Arabian, a highly popular and very versatile saddle horse. On the one hand, Arabians are ridden Western-style in cutting and working cowhorse events, and in trail horse classes, as well as being the most successful breed of all in the endurance riding world; on the other hand they are at home and very successful in the show ring as elegant English Pleasure and Park Horses.

An eye-catching Appaloosa, a breed of spotted horse descended from Spanish stock which is becoming increasingly popular

America today has some of the very best Arabian horses in the world, and the leading breeders have pursued the policy of seeking out the finest Arabians wherever they are to be found and importing them into America. Consequently, the leading bloodlines spring from Desert, English, Polish and Spanish sources, and latterly there have been very selective imports of some Egyptian Arabians.

North America has by far the largest population of Thoroughbreds in the world, and there is a great deal of racing, with most of the action taking place on dirt tracks. But there is tremendous quality as well as great quantity in the American Thoroughbred world, and American-breds have been so successful in top-class international racing in recent years that the best type of American Thoroughbred is now the most sought-after racehorse in the world.

Another racing horse of great speed and courage in North America is the Standardbred harness horse, which can be either trotter or pacer. The breed received its name because, when the American Trotting Register was started in 1871, only horses which could trot or pace a mile (1.6km) in a standard time were accepted for permanent registry. The standard time for the trot was 2·30 minutes and for the pace 2·25 minutes.

The Standardbred got its start when the grey Thoroughbred stallion Messenger was imported into America from Britain in 1788. Messenger was a successful sire of Thoroughbreds, but his real worth was discovered when he was mated with mares of a type that were used for harness racing at country fairs. The offspring proved to be very speedy trotters indeed, and the development of this new breed was considerably helped by Messenger's great-grandson Rysdyk's Hambletonian, which was both an outstanding racer and also a very prepotent sire.

The Standardbred looks somewhat like the Thoroughbred but is heavier-boned, with a longer body, straighter shoulders, flatter ribcage and more steeply sloped quarters. The head is generally not as refined as that of the Thoroughbred, and the nasal profile is often straight or somewhat convex. One special and very useful feature are the nostrils—they can flare open when required to an impressive degree, and this is of great importance when taking in air at speed.

Another very prominent breed in America is the Morgan, a robust yet refined-looking animal

that usually stands between 14 and 15 hands high, and is renowned for its versatility. It is equally at home under Western or Eastern tack, in harness pulling an elegant gig or a heavier cart, jumping fences, or even, when required, lending its strength and its stamina to a really hard day's work on the farm!

All Morgans trace back to one outstanding stallion, the bay horse Figure which was foaled in 1789 in Springfield, Massachusetts, and which later came into the ownership of a schoolteacher named Justin Morgan.

Handsome little Figure was truly a phenomenon—he was an outstanding all-rounder as a performer, winning races both as a ridden galloper and as a trotter in harness, as well as being a champion puller of heavy weights. It wasn't all fun and games for Figure and Justin Morgan though—the incredibly strong, fast, tough stallion often went to work hauling heavy logs as the local wilderness was cleared.

With such a dazzling array of qualities, Figure was much in demand as a sire, and this was when his most amazing virtue came to light: he was almost unbelievably prepotent, 'stamping' nearly every one of his progeny, whether from well-bred mares or poorly bred ones, with his own outstanding type. He was a genetic wonder, and in one generation he had started a whole new breed!

Most Morgans today are bay in colour, and while very robust are also refined in appearance. The head is small and handsome, with large, expressive eyes and well-placed, well-shaped neat ears. The neck is of medium length, well-crested in the stallions, and with a plentiful mane. The shoul-

ders are sloped to provide a smooth action, the back is short, the barrel is well ribbed-out and the chest is deep. The loins are strong, the croup broad and level, and the profuse tail is carried high. This is a horse with much presence, and a very willing, though equable, temperament.

In the early days of the breed, the Morgan was employed mainly as a general-purpose utility and working horse: it was a quality riding horse that could also pull the family buggy to church on Sundays, and take its turn pulling a wagon or plough or snaking out heavy logs from the undergrowth. Nowadays, however, it is best known as a family pleasure horse, a role in which its remarkable versatility makes it very popular.

The Morgan breed also played a large part in the founding of three other very well-known American breeds; the Standardbred (already described above), the Saddlebred and the Tennessee Walking Horse.

The Saddlebred is a close-coupled riding horse of great distinction, with a high head and tail carriage. It is a great favourite in Eastern showrings, where its proud fiery bearing and its spectacular high stepping make it the peacock of American show horses. Saddlebreds are shown as either three-gaited or five-gaited saddle horses, or as fine harness horses. The three-gaited Saddlebred performs walk, trot and canter, all of which are collected and animated. The five-gaited horse is shown at walk, trot and canter, and also at the slow gait and rack. These last two gaits are four-beat gaits, with the hindfoot striking the ground slightly before the forefoot on the same side. The slow gait is a slower version of the rack, and is so spectacular to watch that it can bring

A herd of wild mustangs follow their stallion through the parched country of the Painted Desert

41

even the most enthusiastic and knowledgeable audiences clapping to their feet.

Both slow gait and rack, while inborn to a certain degree in every well-bred Saddlebred, are airs to which the horse must be patiently and carefully trained.

Saddlebreds also make spectacularly successful Parade Horses, and in this sphere of equestrian activity many of the high-stepping Saddlebreds used have the attention-calling palomino coat colour. Their riders wear flamboyant cowboy costumes and sit in heavily ornamented, silvered Western saddles. It is a unique American event which spectators really enjoy seeing.

The American Saddlebred breed was created in horse-knowing Kentucky from a skilful blending of Thoroughbred, Morgan, trotting stock and Naragansett Pacer. The foundation sire of the breed

was a Thoroughbred named Denmark. Today's Saddlebred is a tall horse, standing up to 16·2 hands high. The usual colour is chesnut with flaxen mane and tail, although there are also bays, blacks, greys and palominos.

The Saddlebred has a refined, dry and rather narrow head with large eyes and alert, narrow ears. The neck is long and of a rapier-like elegance, joined to fairly high withers. The Saddlebred's shoulder is very well laid-back, which gives it high-stepping smoothness of action, the back is short and the body rounded and strong. It has a level croup and rounded quarters, and its legs are long and slim, with tendons clearly defined.

Another uniquely American breed, also hailing from the Old South, is the Tennessee Walking Horse. Its origins go back to when wealthy plantation owners set out to breed a smooth-moving,

ground-consuming mount that would allow them and their overseers to spend all day in the saddle with a minimum of fatigue while directing work on their huge estates. They wanted a comfortable ride, good performance, an eager yet equable temperament, and really good looks. By crossing animals with Thoroughbred, Morgan, Saddlebred and Standardbred blood they eventually achieved just this.

Probably the most famous sire in the history of the development of the modern Tennessee Walking Horse was Black Allan, a direct descendant of the great Standardbred Hambletonian. Black Allan was foaled in Kentucky in 1886 and sired three animals that bulk large in the development of this particular breed—the stallions Roan Allan and Hunter's Allan, and the mare Merry Legs.

Tennessee Walking Horses stand 15·2 to 16 hands high, and are compactly and strongly built. The rather long, straight-profiled head of the Tennessee Walker is carried high, is set on a long, powerful neck. The shoulders are long and very well sloped, and this gives the breed its impressive smoothness in action. The back is very short and the quarters are slightly sloped. The horse has a profuse mane and tail, and the tail is carried high. The legs are fine but strong, with powerful hocks well away from the body.

The Walking Horse is amazingly comfortable to ride, since its unique gaits mean that there is no jarring of the rider at any time. These gaits are: the flatfoot walk, a four-beat gait in which the horse seems to glide over the ground, nodding his head slightly; the running walk, which is a much faster and showier version of the flatfoot walk in which the hind feet overstride the front; and the so-called

An exceptionally pretty brood mare leads her sprightly and charming foal for a canter round the paddock

43

'rocking chair' canter, in which the horse takes his forehand forward in a high rolling motion while the hindquarters are held as level as possible.

Nowadays there are two types of Tennessee Walking Horse—show Walkers and pleasure Walkers. The former have more defined action than the latter and to create more spectacular action in front, the front hooves of the show Walker are often weighted and several layers of leather pads are used to build up the hooves themselves.

Latin America

The colourful world of Latin American horsemanship starts off where the southern border of the United States ends, in the exciting and spectacularly beautiful country of Mexico.

The most characteristic horsemen of Mexico are the dashing *charros*, the traditional Mexican cowboys with huge sombreros, tight-fitting short jackets, leg-hugging trousers and beautifully worked spurs. These are very artistic if somewhat severe horsemen, and their lives are built around their prowess in the saddle working half-wild cattle.

They are, without doubt, the greatest experts in the world in roping cattle and horses, and they have a great variety of spectacular catches with their ropes at their command.

While none of the *Anglo*'s riding style has filtered down to the *charro* from above the Rio Grande, the American's Quarter Horse certainly has, and this breed is very popular with the Mexican cowboys for its superb cattle-working qualities.

Thoroughbred racing takes place regularly in Mexico City, and Thoroughbreds are bred on stud farms near the Mexican capital. Andalusians are also seen in Mexico, usually as the parade mounts of the gentlemen horseback bullfighters, the *rejoneadores*, or carrying the wealthy 'gentlemen *charros*' belonging to the exclusive amateur *charros* associations.

In Central and South America there are a considerable number of breeds of horses, but all but a few of them are descendants of the Andalusians imported by the original Spanish settlers. Two distinctive characteristics held in common by many of these breeds are the unmistakable proud bearing inherited from the Andalusian and the special *paso* gait. There are *paso*-type breeds in Peru, Puerto

Rico, Colombia, Cuba, Venezuela, Brazil and the Dominican Republic, and they are all similar in both their general appearance and gait.

Representative of the various *paso* breeds, and certainly the best known outside Latin America, is the Peruvian Paso. A number of these horses have been imported into the United States during recent years, and they are becoming increasingly popular there. The Peruvian Paso stands 13·3 to 15 hands high, with the average being around 14·2 hands. The horses weigh 950 to 975 pounds (430 to 442 kg), and are grey, white, chestnut, bay and black in colour. There are also a few palominos, but piebalds and skewbalds are seldom seen, since these coat colours are very unpopular in Peru, and mares with these markings are never bred from.

The distinctive *paso* gait is basically lateral, with the two legs on one side first being used, and then the two on the other. But, while superficially similar at first glance to a normal pacing gait, the *paso* is actually executed in four separate steps, two by two, the two of each lateral pair being very close in timing. The gait is sometimes described as a 'broken pace', with the rear foot touching the ground a fraction of a second before the forefoot on the same side. The unique, high-kneed action avoids the jarring effect of a true pace, and as a result the Peruvian Paso provides an extremely smooth ride. It also possesses proud, eye-catching bearing, great stamina and a very amenable and friendly temperament.

All this is the result of the unremitting efforts of Peruvian breeders for more than 300 years. The first imported Andalusians were faced with battling their way over Peru's high, rugged mountains, through the humid jungles and across the scorched, waterless deserts, and over the centuries a really tough trail horse was developed as a result of these demanding conditions. At the same time, the Peruvian horsemen selected and bred from only the smoothest-moving animals, paying the strictest attention to the smooth purity of their mounts' natural *paso* gait. Another quality they looked for was a very willing but amenable temperament, and animals with highly strung, nervous, unreliable temperaments were never bred from.

The exemplary temperament of the Peruvian Paso has been a great plus for the breed in the United States, where they are reputed as being very easy to break in. One well-known Western horseman there declared, 'Breaking them to ride or drive is really too easy to be called "breaking". Two saddlings and anyone who can ride at all can ride them. They don't shy, bolt or cut up, making them ideal for older, less active or timorous riders.'

The Peruvian Paso differs considerably in appearance from the parent Andalusian stock from which it is descended, due to the many hundreds of years spent coping with an environment very distinct from that of southern Spain. It is smaller and more wiry, and its legs have become very fine. However, the bones of the Peruvian Paso are particularly dense and strong, and its legs do, in fact, stand up to a tremendous amount of really hard usage over the hard going of its South American homeland.

Peruvian Pasos have abruptly sloping quarters and low-set tails. They are also quite sickle-hocked, with the cannons of their hindlegs sloping forward. This hind limb conformation helps the horse's

The vaqueros *of Mexico are especially famed for their great skill with the lassoo— or* riata, *as they call it*

smooth, steady progression; the rear legs move in a serene gliding action which in turn means that the hindquarters move very little. In the natural *paso* gait the Peruvian Paso's front legs move from the shoulder to reach far forward, and they are raised between 1 foot and 16 inches (300 to 400 mm) from the ground. At the same time, the knee and fetlock joints are flexed, and the hooves are thrown 6 inches (150 mm) or more to the side in a 'dishing' action which is much sought after by the Peruvian horsemen, and which is said to be essential to the

smooth, ground-covering regularity of the Peruvian Paso's famous forward movement.

The breed can also perform the normal pace and the 'marching *paso*', and is able to trot, canter and gallop just like any other horse. Nevertheless, no self-respecting Peruvian rider will permit his mount to perform anything but one of its *paso* gaits. The 'marching *paso*', incidentally, is similar to the pace, but the supports last longer than the suspensions, making the horse look as if it is marching. The print of the rear foot falls in front of the corres-

ponding forefoot print, although not to the same extent as it does in the pace.

The various *paso* breeds of the other Latin American countries mentioned above are very similar in type and action to the Peruvian Paso, and, interestingly enough, horsemen in the United States are working towards blending the best imported members of the various *paso* breeds to develop an ideal horse of this type, through the American Paso Fino Horse Association.

The other most famous of Latin America's horses, the Criollo of Argentina, is also a direct descendant of the Andalusian. However, this internationally renowned stockhorse is very different in appearance from any of the *paso* breeds; it is stocky, very muscular and powerful, and has strong legs with short cannon bones. The Criollo stands about 14 hands high and is close-coupled, with strong loins and quarters. Most Criollos are dun-coloured, but, again in contrast to the *paso* horses, there are many piebalds and skewbalds, which are very popular.

This breed is as tough as it looks, can exist on a minimum of forage, and is remarkably long-lived. Two famous Criollos which were ridden the 13,350 miles (21,500 km) from Buenos Aires, Argentina's

capital, to New York—climbing Andean mountain passes, crossing deserts and slogging through dense jungles on the way—lived until they were more than thirty years old.

Needless to say, the Criollo is the pride of his homeland, and is treasured by the picturesque gauchos (Argentinian cowboys) who ride him after beef cattle on the huge *estancias* of the wide-spreading Pampas.

The Criollo traces back to the first importation of horses into Argentina—when Pedro de Mendoza, the founder of Buenos Aires, shipped in some hundred Andalusians from Spain. When Buenos Aires was attacked by Indians, many of these horses were loosed and escaped into the equine paradise of the Pampas. This new environment suited them so well that within only fifty years their wild descendants had increased from a hundred to several thousand in number.

Hot summers and hard winters added a special brand of toughness to these free-ranging descendants of the Andalusian. And they became especially wily, too, since the Indians hunted them for meat. As the years passed the wild horses became smaller and stockier, and, when captured by the gauchos, they made, after the initial fireworks, both

A shepherd in the Argentinian plains of Patagonia. His pony is the native Criollo; many Argentinian polo ponies are the result of a Criollo-Thoroughbred cross

HRH Prince Philip prepares to send the ball back past his advancing opponent during a hard-fought polo game

excellent cattle horses and strong, hard-working and durable packhorses.

About a century ago, however, a series of breeding mistakes were made which nearly put paid to the excellence of the Criollo: finely bred stallions were imported from the United States and Europe and crossed with the native Criollo mares. The progeny were faster and more refined than the Criollo, but they had less of his toughness, stamina and wiliness.

Luckily, some of the more keen-eyed ranchers saw what was starting to happen to the Criollo, and they decided to work at gaining back the lost ground and at re-establishing the old type of horse. This meant severe selection and considerable culling, but the rigorous exercise of breed reclamation worked.

Argentina boasts a number of top-class Thoroughbred stud farms, and has produced some

racehorses and sires of international class. One of them, the stallion Forli, has done very well as a sire at the top level of the international racing scene in recent years.

The polo pony is another internationally famous Argentinian horse, world renowed for its speed, agility, balance and boldness. These ponies are of a specialized Thoroughbred type which has been developed over many years from the mating of Thoroughbred stallions with native mares.

Argentinian polo ponies are in great demand in North America and Europe, and large numbers of them are exported each year. They are often extremely well schooled, and their trainers frequently journey abroad with them to play as professionals in some of the world's leading polo teams.

Above: the excellent grazing in Virginia produces the sleek condition of these horses

A Tennessee Walking Horse displays his magnificent stride in the show ring

*Above: this horse is an American Standard-bred, a racing horse of great speed and stamina descended from the great Thoroughbred Messenger
Right: Arab horses are now being bred in many parts of the world: this mare and her foal live on a stud farm at Phoenix, Arizona
Opposite above: a horse with Overo markings: black or brown with white patches; those predominantly white with dark patches are called Tobianos
Opposite, below: a group containing Appaloosa horses, originally bred by the Nez Percé Indians from the area around the Palouse river—hence the breed's name*

Above: mares and foals in a wide, sweeping English landscape
Right: a palomino stallion canters proudly around his paddock
Opposite: a Canadian Mountie prepares for a showring appearance; both he and his horse will always be superbly turned out

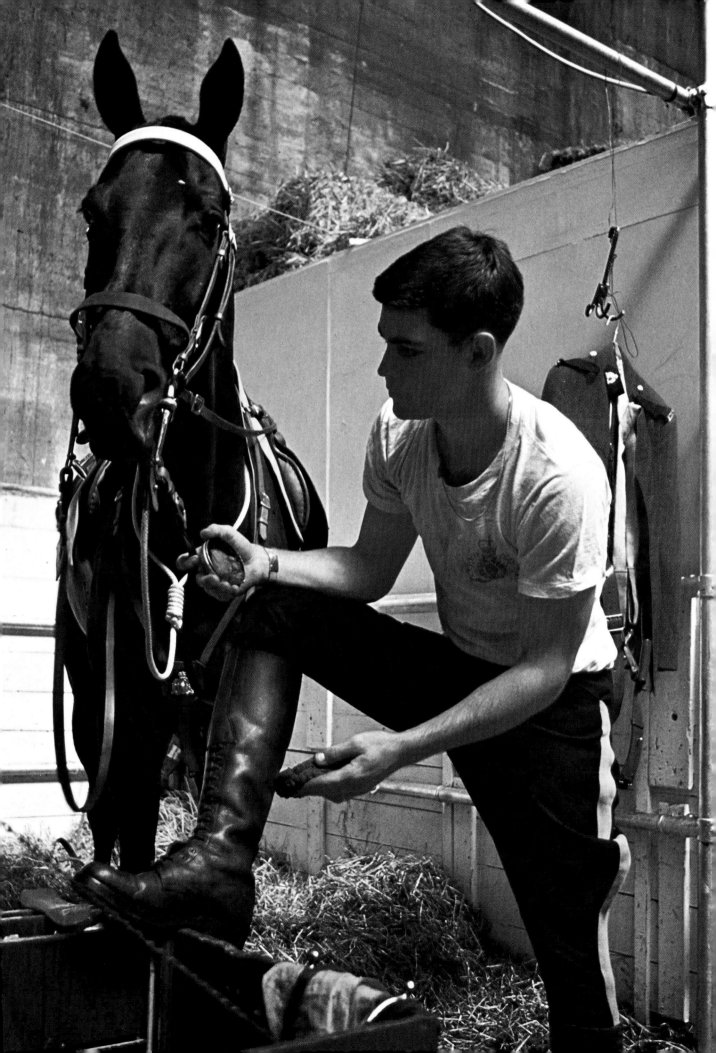

Opposite above, left:
calf-roping is an
important workaday
skill as well as a
spectacular rodeo event
Opposite above, right:
another rodeo
competition, and a
dangerous one: the
cowboy leaps from his
horse to bring the steer
to the ground
Opposite below: putting
their skills into practice,
today's cowboys still
look after vast herds of
cattle, and no machine
can replace them
Left above: a speedy
agile cow pony at work
separating cattle from
the herd
Left below: in saddle
bronc-riding the
cowboy has to stay in the
saddle for ten long-
seeming seconds

Overleaf: the great
American plains once
teemed with buffalo,
which were widely
hunted by the Indians

A good cow pony must be at once fast, agile, and instantly responsive: this Appaloosa is being trained for barrel-racing Opposite: barrel-racing is a fast and thrilling rodeo event and highly popular

Two Brazilian cowboys.
Their equipment, and
their methods of riding
and of working cattle
have Portuguese origins
Opposite: polo also
requires a fast mount
that starts and stops
quickly and is very agile

Overleaf: a Brazilian
cowboy working in a
corral; he needs a fast,
agile, alert mount to
control these Fleet
Brahman cattle

The Horse in Australia

Australia's archetypal horseman is the tall, lean, weatherbeaten stockman of the vast and rugged Outback. He spends the greater part of his life in the saddle, and he sits easily in one, with legs almost completely extended, and feet pushed far forward.

It is a style of riding that a lot of expert foreign horsemen do not much care for when they see it for the first time, but their criticism that the Aussie stockmen ride only one end of their horses tends to die away once they have seen the stockmen in action after half-wild cattle in the timber country. Then the 'ringers' (Australian cowboys) flash between the closely growing trees at breakneck speed after the fleeing cattle, guiding their fast-galloping mounts with the merest touch of a rein on the neck and a miniscule shifting of their weight.

A popular mount for this demanding cattle work is the Australian Stockhorse. This is a fairly recent designation for the horse that used to be known as the Waler, which had a well-deserved fame within Australia and abroad. During World War I more than 120,000 of the tough, game, bush-bred Walers were sent to the Allied armies in Europe, the Middle East, Africa and India. And in the days of the British in India, large numbers of Walers were sent out there as remounts and artillery horses.

The Waler was a hardy horse standing 15 to 15·2 hands high. It was close-coupled, with a well laid-back shoulder, a long neck, a sensible head and excellent legs and feet. The Waler had a deep chest with plenty of heart room, and a strong, well-ribbed-out body.

Knowledge of the origins of the Waler is rather hazy, but it does seem that the basic foundation stock were Cape Horses, imported from South Africa, and themselves a blending of Dutch, Spanish, Barb and Arabian blood. The Australians added a lot of Thoroughbred and some Cob to the tough, strong, even-tempered Cape Horse to produce an exceptional riding animal.

The Walers' descendants, the Australian Stockhorses, are bred on the huge stations in a completely natural way: the stallions run with their bands of mares in very large paddocks, some of which may be more than 10,000 acres (4,000 hectares) in size. Many times a station stallion will be a sound, well-conformed Thoroughbred which has been retired from racing in one of the big cities, and he soon gets used to piloting his band of mares and foals around the bush, seeking out water and grass wherever it can be found, and under all sorts of varying climatic conditions.

Australian Stockhorses are often not broken in until they are four or five years old. By then they are fully developed in wind and limb, and really tough and independent after all those years ranging the virtually untrammeled bushland. So when it is time to introduce them to bridle and saddle and rider, extremely knowledgeable horsemen with a fair dose of courage are required for the task.

They drive the wild-eyed, plunging horses one by one into a high-fenced and stoutly built round yard, where the animals are lassooed, hobbled and 'sacked out' with a sack, a saddle blanket or an old shirt attached to the tip of a long pole. Once a horse has had enough sessions of this handling, it will allow itself to be rubbed over, and in time a saddle can be girthed on to it. Then progress is made in easy stages until a rider can climb into the saddle. Nevertheless, for all the patient, skilful handling that has preceded this moment, there is no surety

Opposite: manoeuvring a herd of unruly steers

that the bush horse won't explode into a head-plunging arc of fury as soon as he feels a man on his back for the very first time!

Once a horse has been broken in it will join the group of stockhorses running together in the 'home' paddock or 'horse' paddock on the station. Every day that there is horse work to be done, this unshod, ungroomed bunch of horses, which subsist entirely on grass, are brought into the stockyards in the early morning at a gallop. As they plunge around the high-fenced stockyard in a cloud of fine dust the 'ringers' select their mounts for the day, catch them —sometimes with a lassoo—saddle up and climb aboard. And there may well be fireworks for a few moments!

Another famous Australian bush horse is the brumby, the wild horse. Brumbies are descended from former saddle stock which strayed and went wild, and they are tough and as sharp-sensed as deer. It is very difficult to get close to brumbies in the bush, let alone catch them, but some few expert and very hard-riding horsemen do manage to capture the wild horses by chasing them into skilfully concealed stockyards.

With a workaday background such as that described above, it is small wonder that the Australian stockman turns to the contests of the rodeo arena for his leisure enjoyment. And it is at the rodeos that the Australian Stockhorses can be seen

in action in the uniquely Australian competition of campdrafting. In this event a rider has to separate a large bullock from a group of cattle, then drive it at the gallop around a large course marked out with upright poles. Often the horse is used to shoulder the bullock over in the direction in which the rider wants the beast to go, and at all times the rider atop his long-striding stockhorse must stay very close to the fleeing animal. If the bullock should suddenly switch direction and cut under the horse's neck, man and mount can be in for an unpleasant tumble.

Another breed of horse to be seen at the Australian rodeos today in ever-increasing numbers is America's Quarter Horse. This fast-starting, fast-

These three photographs show Australian stockmen at work and play

stopping and quick-turning cattlehorse is a top mount for rodeo contests such as bull-dogging, in which two riders pursue a fleeing steer and one of them drops on to it at the gallop, grasps its horns and wrestles it to the ground. The Quarter Horse is also a very talented roping horse and outstanding in cutting competitions, two contests which have been 'imported' from the United States.

America's spotted Appaloosa is also bred in Australia in small numbers, as is the peacock-necked, high-stepping American Saddlebred.

At a new high peak of popularity in Australia is the Arabian, as a pleasure horse, a show horse and a mount for the gruelling endurance rides staged over rugged bushland courses. Much of the original breeding stock of the Arabian in Australia was imported from England, but in recent years there has been considerable interest in Arabians from America, particularly those carrying Egyptian bloodlines.

Where the Arabian has made a special niche for himself in Australia is in endurance riding. The most important endurance riding event is the Quilty 100-Mile Endurance Ride, which takes place over very testing going in the Blue Mountains inland from Sydney, and the Arabian staked his claim as an outstanding endurance horse from the very first running of the contest in 1966. The winner then was the blaze-faced Arabian stallion Shalawi, ridden bareback by his owner Gabriel Stecher. In fact, Shalawi made such an impact upon the world of Australian endurance riding that a well-known contest is named after him— it is the 50-mile (80 km) Shalawi Memorial, which is held near Melbourne, capital city of the State of Victoria.

Racing is an extremely popular sport in Australia, which boasts many beautiful racecourses with superb facilities for patrons. Australian Thoroughbreds are of good quality, and from time to time a champion of international class is produced. In recent years a number of these top-class Australian racehorses have ended up in the United States as sires. But probably the single most famous product of the Australian racecourse is the Australian jockey—Aussie race riders are renowned throughout the world for their skill and timing, and they have had great success riding in the British Isles and Europe.

Most training of racehorses in Australia takes place at the racecourses in the early morning, with the horses working out on concentric tracks inside the racecourse proper. For much of the time that his charges are working, the Australian trainer will be using a stopwatch—and it is this habit of riding to the watch, according to many, which gives Australian jockeys their tremendous sense of timing.

The biggest event in Australia's racing year is undoubtedly the 2-mile (3·2 km) Melbourne Cup, during the running of which the entire nation virtually grinds to a halt in order to watch the great race on television or to listen to it on the radio.

A most unusual and very colourful type of racing can be witnessed in Australia at the picnic race meetings. These events are staged in the Outback, and amateur riders on grass-fed Thoroughbreds vie with each other around primitive bushland racetracks. There are special races for lady riders, and in many places there are also races for the Aboriginal stockmen who play such a large part in working the enormous herds of beef cattle

on the Outback stations. Picnic race meetings last for two, three or more days, with plenty of eating, drinking, dancing and laughing, as well as the slightly more serious business of racing.

The breeding of Thoroughbreds is a growth activity in Australia, with some excellent stallions being imported from overseas—mainly England and America—to stand at stud. Brood mares are rarely stabled on stud farms Down Under, even for foaling. They are allowed to roam freely in large paddocks all year long, and a great many of them foal quite alone in a quiet gully or hidden in some scrub. Some of the more progressive stud farms do, however, have special small foaling paddocks which are floodlit at night so that watch can be kept for any mare which may experience difficulties during foaling and need expert assistance in order to deliver her valuable foal safely.

Thoroughbreds are also used in Australia for showjumping and eventing, and in show ring hack events. There are contests for 10 stone (63·5 kg), 12 stone (76·2 kg), and 14 stone (88·9 kg) hacks, ladies' and gentlemen's hacks, educated hacks, open classes and also for pairs and teams. Hacks in Australia, are, however, quite different from the hacks that one sees in British show rings: they are usually tall

Thoroughbreds, perhaps 16 to 16·2 hands in height, and many of them are retired racehorses which have been patiently re-schooled by their devoted riders.

In the hack event the judge first looks over the horses as they walk, trot and canter in a large circle around him, then he calls them in, lines them up and asks them to do their individual 'shows' one by one. There is much emphasis on the figure eight at the canter, with a very smooth change of lead being looked for.

Thoroughbreds are also very much in demand as polo ponies in the country districts where this exciting sport is popular and there are facilities to play it. Often the infield of the local racecourse is used as the polo field. In some areas, where the game has been played for many years, the standard is very high, and a number of Australian polo teams and individual players have won considerable fame abroad.

Another fast-moving sport in which smaller Thoroughbreds and animals carrying plenty of Thoroughbred blood are popular is polocrosse. This is an Australian invention which has all the thrills and action of polo at only a fraction of its cost. A player needs only one mount for the entire game, as opposed to polo, where he needs several. In polo-

Action – and dust! At a picnic race meeting in the Australian Outback

crosse the ball is picked up with a small net at the end of a long stick, and then is carried or thrown. The sport takes place in a much more restricted area than polo, and the ponies do not have to gallop so far, which is why a player can get by with only one mount.

Trotting and pacing races are very popular in Australia, and are staged at night at floodlit city tracks and at the many agricultural shows. In the big cities the trotting tracks are beautifully appointed installations featuring many amenities, including glass-fronted restaurants where fans can eat as they follow the racing.

At the agricultural shows the trotters and pacers battle it out around circular quarter-mile (400-metre) tracks, with the audience ringing the arena able to watch every stride of the action closely.

A visit to a large Australian show is a thrilling experience for the horse fancier, since there are so many breeds now represented Down Under. In-

hand classes are staged for Thoroughbreds, Arabians, Quarter Horses, Appaloosas, American Saddlebreds, Palominos, Australian Stockhorses, the various breeds of ponies, and even, in some places, for Andalusians.

Driving classes are popular, too, at the bigger shows, and there are competitions for Hackney horses and ponies as well as general-purpose driving animals of mixed breeding.

The heavy horses also have their place in

Australia, although not much used for farming in its highly mechanized agriculture, and the spectacular Clydesdale is a particular favourite of the show ring crowds.

These beautiful Thoroughbred mares and foals on an Australian stud live outside all the year round

71

The Art of Riding

At its most accomplished and refined, riding moves from a skilful sporting activity into the realms of pure art. Today this ultimate level of equestrian accomplishment is seen in very few places, and by far the most famous is the world-renowned Spanish Riding School in Vienna.

There the beautiful white Lipizzaners move with stately grace in a unique spectacle held in the world's most magnificent riding hall. Alone, in pairs, trios, or in quadrilles of four, eight or twelve, the superbly schooled stallions and their erect uniformed riders thrill spectators as they perform high school airs on and above the ground.

Besides Vienna, there is the cavalry school at Saumur in France, whose élite *Cadre Noir* are superbly graceful high school horsemen. This handful of black-uniformed riders proudly keep up the tradition of *haute école* in the country which was once the leading exponent of the art. There are also a few outstanding individual high school riders of the calibre of, for example, Nuno Oliviera of Portugal.

Worthy of attention, too, is the recently formed Andalusian School of Equestrian Art at Jerez de la Frontera, Spain, which is seeking to re-establish the traditions of the high school riding on Andalusian stallions which flourished in southern Spain hundreds of years ago.

These relatively few riders with their magnificently trained mounts are the last guardians of an art which goes back to before 400 BC. It was in 400 BC that the earliest surviving book about the art of riding was written by the Greek general Xenophon. It is a masterpiece of its kind—clearly written, packed with valuable information for the advanced rider, and based on the premise that 'Anything forced and misunderstood can never be beautiful.'

Xenophon also quotes from an even earlier book, by Simon of Athens, which has since been lost: 'If a dancer were forced by whip and spikes, he would be no more beautiful than a horse trained under similar conditions.'

With the fall of the Greek and Roman Empires, followed by the Barbarian invasion and the development of the armoured knight on his heavy warhorse, the art of riding went into eclipse. Its re-emergence was principally due to the invention of gunpowder. Firearms and the crossbow put the heavily armoured knight and his lumbering giant of a mount out of business, and suddenly the skilful rider on a disciplined, fast and agile horse came back into his own.

It was in the city of Naples that the first great schools of the re-emergent art of riding were founded. By the curve of the city's spectacular bay Count Fiaschi opened his school, and in 1539 wrote a book on what he called 'the secret weapon'—the art of the skilful rider on a highly trained horse. He was followed by another nobleman, Grisone, who had studied Xenophon's book in great detail, and who based much of his own instruction upon its classic principles.

The most famous of Grisone's numerous pupils was Pignatelli, and writings of the time describe how he and his pupils, sitting deep, erect and quiet on their horses, with the reins in one hand and a sword in the other, were able to make the horses start, stop, whirl, rear and sidestep with slight movements of hands, heels and body that would go undetected in the heat of battle and therefore be of great advantage. From this eminently practical background, it would appear, initially derives the tradition of the use of almost imperceptible aids in

Fig. 16.

the advanced horsemanship of today.

Pignatelli's own best-known pupil was de Pluvinel, who later became riding master to Louis XIII of France. He followed the basic pattern of Pignatelli's method, but increasingly substituted the use of force with much more humane techniques. This was a major breakthrough in classical equitation, and from then on France became the centre of Europe's high school horsemanship, with Italy gradually declining in importance.

Meanwhile, during the latter part of the sixteenth century, the foundations of a durable edifice of equestrian skill were being laid in Vienna, with the building of a riding hall in the Josefsplatz and the importation of the Andalusian horses from which the Lipizzaners were to descend. Germany's nobility, too, was deeply interested in the art of riding, and a famous book about its principles was published there in 1588 by von Loehneysen.

Even England, the traditional home of open-air sporting horsemanship, and never very taken with the airs of the covered riding school, in the seventeenth century produced one of the greatest high school masters of all time. He was William Cavendish, Duke of Newcastle, who published a famous book on horsemanship in 1667. Although reputed to be hard on his horses and sternly unwavering in his demand for the utmost obedience from them, he wrote that the horse 'hath imagination, memory and judgement; I work on this, which is why my horses go so well.'

But it was in France that high school horsemanship was attaining its greatest heights. 1733 saw the publication of the epoch-making work that the late Colonel Alois Podhajsky, famed former Director of the Spanish Riding School, termed 'the most revolutionary book on riding of all times.' It was *Ecole de Cavalerie* by François Robichon de la

An 18th century engraving showing the Duke of Newcastle astride a superbly trained high school horse

73

Le Pas.   *Le Trot.*

Guérinière and, after many of the long-winded works that had preceded it, it was remarkable for its clarity and apparent simplicity.

De la Guérinière prospered from his riding and instructing skills, and he became director of the riding school at the Tuileries, which had been empty since the Royal Stables were relocated at Versailles. And there he remained, the shining light of French classical equitation in its fullest flower, until his death in 1751. A lasting and living monument to the equestrian genius of de la Guérinière is the 'complete suppling movement' of the shoulder-in, which he developed to a perfection that has never been surpassed.

At the same time as de la Guérinière was riding and writing and teaching in Paris, a whole group of brilliant horsemen were in action at the Royal School of Versailles. There was de Nestier, nicknamed 'The Great Silent One', who had taught Louis XV to ride; de Salvert, director of the Great Stables; and the imaginative Marquis de la Bigne, who once took a whole hour to cross Versaille's *Place d'Armes* at an unbroken canter, his mount bitted only with a silken thread!

However, the French Revolution was to change the whole course of the country's equitation as much as it did its other institutions. In the aftermath of the far-reaching political changes, France's horsemanship became much more orientated towards essentially practical ends, in particular the training of mount and man for cavalry combat. It was in this ferment that the famous School of Versailles disappeared forever—its role as France's University of Equitation gradually being assumed by the cavalry school at Saumur. This establishment, still flourishing today, was principally intended for training cavalry officers. At the same time, however, it also kept alive the flame of classical *haute école*, which was and is practised with great skill by its small corps of instructors, the *écuyers* of Saumur's *Cadre Noir*.

In Vienna, however, there were no such changes, and the Spanish Riding School continued in its own inimitable time-honoured way, keeping alive for future generations the airs and style of the eighteenth century. Playing a fundamental part in the Spanish School's conservative role was Max Ritter von Weyrother, Head Rider at the School during the early part of the nineteenth century.

French high school riding still had one more genius to give to the world, however—François Baucher, a butcher's son who first wanted to become *écuyer en chef* at the cavalry school at Saumur, and who, when frustrated in this ambition, travelled round Europe riding spectacular high school in various circuses. Baucher's beautifully balanced mounts performed the *passage* with such short strides that they obtained incredibly high steps. Baucher also invented the flying change of leg at every stride, which, although at first bitterly attacked by the classicists, today forms an indispensable part of the highest-level dressage tests, and has even been incorporated into the programme of the Spanish Riding School.

From Scotland in the nineteenth century came James Fillis, a brilliant high school horseman who spent much of his life in France and Russia. He also performed in the circus from time to time, and was renowned for his highly artificial airs; his horses, for example, could canter backwards in a state of perfect collection on three legs! This was a very long way from the sober conception of the classical high

Le Galop désuni du devant à droite. *Le Galop désuni du derriere à droite.*

school, which, however, has continued on into the latter half of the twentieth century and can be seen today in the few places mentioned at the beginning of this chapter.

High School Riding and Training

The performances of the Spanish Riding School in Vienna display high school riding at its most classical. After a relatively low-key beginning to the programme, when the young stallions new to the School are ridden in simple, straightforward movements, a single fully-trained stallion is ridden into the marvellous riding hall to perform impeccable high school. He will seem to float above the ground in the majestic *passage*, dance gracefully upon the spot in the *piaffe*, pirouette with rhythmic precision, and perform the flying change of leg at every stride—all to an appropriate musical accompaniment.

After this virtuoso exhibition, other highly trained stallions work superbly together in the *Pas de Deux* or *Pas de Trois*, their splendid appearance matched only by their great precision.

Then comes the 'Work in Hand', which demonstrates how the muscular stallions are prepared for the so-called 'exercises above the ground', working from the *piaffe* alongside the wall and between the pillars to the *levade*, the *capriole* and the *courbette* in hand.

In the *levade* the horse raises his forehand from the ground, his forelegs neatly tucked under his body, and remains motionless with all his weight delicately balanced and supported by his lowered hindquarters. The *capriole* is a spectacular stag-like

leap high into the air, concluded by a slashing kick back with the hind legs. This is the most difficult of all the exercises above the ground, and can be taught only after a series of related exercises leading up to it have been mastered by the horse.

The *courbette* consists of a series of leaps on the hind legs without the front legs touching the ground. It develops from the dancing-on-the-spot *piaffe*, which in turn becomes a *levade*, from which the stallion launches himself into the forward leap which ends each time with the animal again in the position of the *levade*. Some stallions can perform as many as five leaps one after another in this difficult exercise!

After the display of 'Work in Hand' has been concluded, a single Lipizzaner enters the expanse of the shining white riding hall, driven in long reins with his traditionally dressed handler walking very close to his hind legs. Amazingly, guided only by the reins, this stallion will perform all the airs and exercises that have been shown by the ridden stallions, and the trainer's subtlety of touch and command is truly phenomenal.

Next the spectator is treated to a never-to-be-forgotten exhibition by a number of stallions of airs above the ground—but this time the horses are ridden, without stirrups, as they perform *levades, ballotades, courbettes* and *caprioles* in response to the almost imperceptible urgings of their riders.

The process that leads to such perfection is a long and arduous one for both mount and man. The young Lipizzaner stallions are brought from the stud farm to Vienna only when they are four years old—by this age most successful racehorses would have retired or be competing for their last season. However, the Lipizzaner is a late-maturing breed, and in fact the horses do not reach their full physical

Illustrations from the epoch-making Ecole de Cavalerie *written by de la Guérinière, in 1733*

75

One of the most magnificent of all the advanced movements of haute école, *the* ballotade; *the* capriole *is a similar 'air above the ground', but the horse kicks its hind legs out behind at the climax of the leap*

development until they are all of seven years old. For this reason their early training is taken very slowly, and during his first year at the Spanish Riding School the young stallion is asked to do very little—the objective is to gain his confidence, to make him obedient and to strengthen him and improve his suppleness, efficiency and stamina. At the end of this first year of training, which begins with a period on the lunge rein, the Lipizzaner stallion should have learned to go straight and forward under his rider at walk, trot and canter. He should also, as a result of the development of his muscles and improvement in his bearing and movements, have become more beautiful.

It is very interesting to note that during the first year of training at the Spanish Riding School the horse is ridden by young, inexperienced riders. This course is followed for several reasons: a younger rider will generally be lighter and less of a strain on a young horse's back, and inexperienced riders will be less demanding on their mounts than experienced riders would be. However, as soon as the second

stage of training begins, the inexperienced riders are taken off the young stallions and are replaced with seasoned men with great knowledge and physical ability. This is because the second stage of training is the most important one, with much repetitious work that requires skilled, consistent trainers.

The first step is to get the horse to take a correct contact with the bit and to work continually on improving the animal's 'collection' (i.e. the proud, balanced and lively way in which the fully trained high school horse carries himself). During the first stage of training the stallion will have been ridden in the rising trot, but during the second stage he will be introduced to the sitting trot, in which the rider does not rise at all from the saddle, since this gives him a deeper, more balanced seat, and allows him to feel the horse's movements much better.

There will be work on the large circle at walk, trot and canter, and much attention is paid to the seemingly simple business of passing through the corners of the school. In fact, it can be very difficult to ride through a corner correctly, describing an arc

that is an exact quarter of a circle, the diameter of which is not greater than 6 yards (5·5 metres), with the body of the horse bent so that its spine corresponds to this arc. A great deal of time is also spent on riding simple turns and small circles, and always there is the unrelenting search for improvement, even in these uncomplicated movements, since all this training is laying the basis for the demanding high school work of the years to come. The figures then start to become somewhat more complicated, with the horse learning the change within the circle and the figure of eight within the circle, as well as half voltes and changes.

The stallion will now have reached the stage when he can be introduced to lateral work, in which he steps not only forward but sideways as well. He starts with the shoulder-in, the basic training for all lateral work, which is also a suppling exercise used to make the horse straight. Eventually, after mastering the shoulder-in and other basic lateral exercises, he will be introduced to the half pass, in which he moves obliquely forward with much impulsion and under perfect control, and also the full pass, a completely sideways movement. As a final preparation for the third stage of training, the true high school, the Lipizzaner stallion will be taught the turn on the

haunches, in which the forehand describes a half circle around the hind legs, and the rein back.

In the third stage of training there is a continuous striving after perfection. The trainer must have a complete grasp of the task confronting him, and, while consistently asking the most that his mount has to offer at any given stage, he must also be understanding and sympathetic. A rare blend of character, technique, talent and experience is required to develop a horse from this already advanced stage to the spectacular fullness of high school.

Now the really advanced work begins: the flying change of leg, the counter canter and work on two tracks at the canter, leading finally to one of the most difficult movements of all, the pirouette, which requires much impulsion, perfect balance and great proficiency.

The peak of the high school stallion's training in the airs on the ground is reached when he learns to perform the *passage* and *piaffe*, the two highly spectacular airs based on the trot. They can be performed correctly only after the long period of training has been completed, and to execute *passage* and *piaffe* properly a horse must be strong and well-developed, in perfect balance, and totally without

The head carriage and lofty movement of these young Lipizzaners are qualities inherent in the breed

any kind of tension or strain.

Once the Lipizzaner stallion has been schooled to this peak of perfection, the School authorities take a long hard look at his natural abilities to see whether he is suitable for training in the performance of one or more of the airs above the ground. Only a few of the horses do, in fact, have the required talent as well as the intelligence that is needed for this very demanding work. And many of those chosen for performing airs above the ground will be limited to just one or two of the difficult exercises. Certainly, none of the stallions can perform all of them. Horses with quieter temperaments will be more suited to the statuesque *levade*; those with more spirited natures and the requisite balance and muscular proficiency will be more at home soaring high in the *capriole* leap. Yet others will fit some-

where in between in the highly controlled alternate squatting and leaping of the *courbette*.

Training the riders at the Spanish Riding School begins with teaching them to acquire a deep, graceful and so-called 'independent' seat—independent, that is, of the need to hang on to the reins at any stage to retain balance. This is achieved by having the novice horsemen ride without stirrups on a horse circling around an instructor at the end of a lunge rein. The young rider learns to sit properly at walk, trot and canter, and also performs all manner of mounted exercises to develop balance and suppleness. This initial part of a rider's training at the School usually takes from about six months to a year.

During the latter stages of this training, the student will also begin to ride a fully schooled stallion,

in order to become gradually established in independent work. At the Spanish Riding School, once he has acquired an independent seat on the lunge rein, he will be put on a fully trained horse because it is believed that this is the best and fastest way for him to acquire the feel of a correctly performed movement. The horse will, in a sense, train the young rider—who, once he has mastered his art, will in turn school young horses, turning the training wheel full circle.

In fact, there are two different objectives in training a high school rider at the Spanish School: the first is to educate him so that he can ride a fully trained stallion and show all its airs with brilliance, which will take from two to four years; the second, which will take from four to six years, is to learn to train a horse, beginning with a raw recruit and ending with the perfect mount of the upper level of high school.

Dressage

A modern offshoot of classical horsemanship is the increasingly popular art-sport of competitive dressage, in which the horses' performances are judged according to the correctness of execution, obedience and style they demonstrate. The tests are of varying difficulty, depending on the standard that the horses taking part have reached, and the most advanced tests include the high school airs of *passage* and *piaffe*. In order to perform at all creditably in a dressage test, a horse must be light in hand, obedient and supple.

Dressage is far more popular in West Germany than in any other country, and so it is no surprise that the Germans have more strength in this particular horse activity than anyone else. Not only are there hundreds of riders in West Germany capable of showing horses in the very highest tests, there is a great popular interest in dressage, with enthusiasts numbered in thousands. A top level dressage contest will nearly always 'play' to a capacity audience formed of really knowledgeable fans.

There seem to be several reasons why Germany has taken such a great interest in dressage and produced so very many outstanding horses and riders. First of all, there is the historical background of the many German courts, most of which had their own skilled *manège* riders in the classical manner. Then there is the German passion for precise form and order, which finds equestrian expression in the accuracy, obedience and control demanded by the dressage test from both horse and rider. And finally, there is enough wealth in modern West Germany to be able to afford to buy, train and exhibit top-level dressage horses.

Some of the most successful West German dressage riders are very wealthy individuals who keep as many as fifteen or twenty horses in training at a time in palatial privately owned riding establishments. They will have two or three full-time professional trainers preparing their mounts, and they are also well able to take care of the large overheads incurred in taking their horses to the various competitions. However, being a top German dressage rider is not a matter of wealth alone—as well as having the money for horses and trainers,

There is a great precision and accuracy in this extended trot, executed by a competitor in the Grand Prix class at the Dressage World Championship held at Copenhagen in 1974

Dr Reiner Klimke, one of West Germany's leading dressage exponents in action on the Hanoverian Dux
Below: a beautiful Lipizzaner stallion from the Spanish Riding School in Vienna

Opposite: healthy, happy mares and foals in a sun-scorched Australian paddock

you must also have a great deal of innate talent and a tremendous amount of dedication.

Russia also produces world-class dressage riders, and in the USSR the State provides the financial backing. Other countries where dressage has had a successful history are Sweden (which breeds the horses probably most suited to dressage) and Switzerland, whose cavalries provided the facilities for training accomplished dressage horses and riders. France, too, has in the past given some great dressage performers to the competitive arena from its famed *Cadre Noir* of the School of Saumur. However, interest in dressage is very restricted in France today, although recently several really good riders have been seen in action.

Interest in dressage in Britain has traditionally not been great, but it has increased considerably during the last 25 years, and there now exists a small group of excellent dressage riders with highly schooled mounts.

There has also recently been a sudden dramatic surge of interest in dressage in the United States and Canada, countries which, given the energy and dedication of their riders, plus the considerable wealth available for horses and trainers as well as study abroad, may mean that North America is well on the way to becoming a force to be reckoned with on the international dressage scene. The fresh impetus this would undoubtedly give to the unique art of dressage is certainly something all horse-lovers and spectators will welcome.

Above: a dramatic picture of a hurdle race at Melbourne, Australia. Inside the turf course a dirt training track can also be seen

Right: Australian rodeo sports are an extension of the everyday working life of the stockmen

*An impressive view of
the Grand Parade,
climax of the Easter
Show held in Sydney*

*Below: in Australia,
horses are still much
used on the sheep stations
Opposite: a New South
Wales sheep farmer with
his horse and wagon out
droving sheep*

*Right: racing for the
finish at a picnic race
meeting in the
Australian Outback
Below: an Aboriginal
stockman herds cattle
through the Outback
landscape
Opposite: hard-riding
and fearless, the
Australian Aborigines
make good stockmen*

*A magnificent stallion
gives an impressive
display on a stud at
Celle, West Germany
Opposite: a complete
contrast: the refined
power of the Lipizzaner*

*Right: another beautiful
Lipizzaner; this one is
performing the passage,
while being driven in
long reins
Below: this figure is
believed to represent
Alexander the Great, an
outstanding horseman
Opposite: members of
Vienna's famous
Spanish Riding School
entering the riding hall*

Opposite: the pesade, *another* haute école *movement requiring great skill on the part of both horse and rider*
Left: a smooth, elegant performance of dressage at the Olympic Games by Mrs Jennie Loriston-Clarke and Kadett
Below: the sumptuous architecture of the Spanish Riding School's hall forms a spectacular background for equestrian activities

The proud magnificence of a quality Portuguese bullfighting horse, another valuable and highly trained type of horse
Opposite: the extraordinary grace of a beautifully trained dressage horse is brought out by Liselotte Linsenhoff, riding Piaff for West Germany in the World Championships at Copenhagen

Thoroughbred Racing in Europe and America

Europe

As we have already seen in 'The Horse in Europe', the 'founding fathers' of the Thoroughbred racehorse were three Eastern stallions imported into England, the Darley Arabian, the Byerley Turk and the Godolphin Barb. Every Thoroughbred in the world today is descended in direct male line from one of them.

The blaze-faced, prick-eared Darley Arabian was purchased in 1704 in Aleppo for James Darley by his merchant son. He had been bred by the renowned Anazeh horsemen living on the edge of the Syrian desert, and is said to have been splendidly conformed and to have had three white stockings. He became the paternal great-great-grandsire of the famous Eclipse.

The Byerley Turk was originally a cavalry charger; acquired by Captain Robert Byerley when fighting against the Turks in Hungary, he carried Byerley (then a colonel in charge of the Sixth Dragoon Guards under King William of Orange) into action in the Battle of the Boyne in 1690. When they returned to England, the Byerley Turk first went to stud in Co. Durham and then was sent to Yorkshire. He achieved lasting fame as the paternal grandsire of Herod.

The Godolphin Barb, which was bred in Morocco and given by the ruler of that country to King Louis XIV of France, was brought to England from Paris by Edward Coke. Legend has it that Coke discovered the stallion in the shafts of a cart in the streets of the French capital! When Coke died in 1733 he left the horse to a friend, who in turn sold it to Lord Godolphin who had inherited all of Coke's mares. The Godolphin Barb was the paternal grandsire of Matchem, the famous sire of winners of more than £150,000.

However, while the Darley Arabian, the Byerley Turk and the Godolphin Barb are the only male lines which have lasted until today in direct descent from sire to son, a number of other imported stallions have played important parts in the development of the Thoroughbred. Two of the best-remembered are the grey Alcock Arabian and the Leedes Arabian. Another famous horse was the Darcy White Turk, the sire of Hautboy, whose name appears all of nine times in the pedigree of Eclipse, while the Darley Arabian's name is listed only once.

Racing as an organized sport really got under way in England with the restoration of the Stuart Monarchy in 1660. King Charles II was an ultra-keen racing fan and a very accomplished race-rider himself. James I and Charles I had used the Suffolk village of Newmarket as a hunting box, but Charles II made it into the centre of racing. He would go to Newmarket for weeks at a time to see racing and to take part in races on the famous heath.

Queen Anne started racing at Ascot in 1711, and while she was on the throne nine Arabian, eight Barb and seven Turkoman stallions were imported. Playing a role of fundamental importance in the development of racing at this time was Tregonwell Frampton, known as 'the father of the English Turf'. He had been made Supervisor of the Royal Racehorses at Newmarket by William of Orange, and he was paid £1,000 a year to provide ten racehorses and ten lads to ride them. In those early days before the founding of the Jockey Club, Tregonwell Frampton's word on racing matters carried almost the weight of law.

Opposite: a herd of Lipizzaner mares and foals with the castle of Piber in the background. The Spanish Riding School trains stallions only from the Piber Stud Farm

The Jockey Club was founded twenty years after Frampton died, and the Duke of Cumberland, the second son of King George II, was the first member of the Royal Family to be elected to it. The duke was commander of the army that defeated Bonnie Prince Charlie's Highlanders at the Battle of Culloden, and he was also one of the first great Thoroughbred breeders of history, for his stud produced both Herod and Eclipse.

Herod was foaled in 1758 and was one of the fastest racehorses of his time. At stud he sired the winners of more than £200,000, including High-flyer, a racehorse that was never beaten and was later purchased by Richard Tattersall, founder of the famous firm of bloodstock auctioneers of that name. Highflyer was a very successful sire, and when he died Tattersall had engraved on the stone above the horse's grave, 'Here lieth the perfect and beautiful symmetry of the much-lamented High-flyer, by whom and by his wonderful offspring the celebrated Tattersall acquired a noble fortune, but was not ashamed to admit it.'

In 1750 the Duke of Cumberland acquired a brown yearling colt called Marske, whose dam was a grand-daughter of the Darley Arabian. At stud Marske was at first not popular, and his chances of siring good stock were extremely restricted because of the poor quality of the mares to which he was bred. However, eventually he was mated with a good mare named Spiletta, a grand-daughter of the Godolphin Barb, and she produced one of the greatest racehorses of all time. This was Eclipse, foaled on April 1, 1764, a day that was notable for an eclipse of the sun.

Eclipse first raced in May 1769, nearly four years after the death of his breeder. He won this first contest easily, and during the next two years he competed 26 times and was never beaten. When he went to stud Eclipse was also enormously success-ful—he sired 344 winners of more than £158,000 in stakes.

During the period that Herod and Eclipse were making history on the racecourse, important changes were occurring on the Turf, many of them detailed in the various Racing Calendars published by John Pound, William Fawconer, William Tutin and Newcastle solicitor James Weatherby. It was the Calendar produced by Weatherby, however, which won the day and became established as the authentic record of the English Turf.

Until the last thirty years of the eighteenth century horses were not usually raced until they were four or five years old. The inauguration of the July Stakes at Newmarket for two-year-olds in 1785 was

Racing in the late 18th century at Ascot, which is still one of Britain's most important and fashionable racecourses

therefore a momentous step, and races for youngsters of this age soon proliferated. One important proviso that was often included in the conditions for races for two-year-olds at that time was that animals sired by Eclipse and Highflyer should carry an extra 3 pounds (1·4 kg)!

The most far-reaching single event influencing the future of the English Turf was the founding of the Jockey Club, which came to wield tremendous power over the conduct of racing throughout the country. The Jockey Club originally met at a Pall Mall inn called 'The Star and Garter', and later the members gathered at The Corner, Hyde Park, where public relations-minded horse auctioneer Richard Tattersall put a room and a skilled chef at their disposal. The Jockey Club finally moved to its own premises in Newmarket in the 1750s.

Sir Charles Bunbury was the leading member of the Jockey Club during its early days. He was its President for more than forty years, during which time he was the owner of Diomed, the colt that won the first Derby, Eleanor, the first filly to win the Derby and the Oaks, and Smolensko, the first colt to win the Derby and the Two Thousand Guineas. In

a stern age, Sir Charles Bunbury was remarkable in that he never allowed his jockeys or stable lads to use a whip on his horses because he believed that treatment of this kind would make them unruly and even vicious.

In 1779 Edward Stanley, the 12th Earl of Derby, and some friends organized a race at Epsom for three-year-old fillies. They named it after Lord Derby's Epsom home 'The Oaks', and it was so successful that the following summer they inaugurated a race for three-year-old colts, and called it the Derby.

The winner of the first Derby at Epsom was Sir Charles Bunbury's Diomed, a muscular chesnut which stood at Bunbury's stud for sixteen years following his notable victory. But he was not a success as a stallion in England, and at the advanced age of twenty he was sold for a low sum to an American breeder. In America he lived on until he was thirty, and also founded the first great line of American racehorses.

The Derby and the Oaks were in fact the second and third Classic races to be established. Earlier, in 1776, the St Leger had been organized at

Coming up to the finish, every muscle stretched in the final attempt to be first past the post

Doncaster for the first time by Colonel Anthony St Leger. The pattern of Britain's five Classic races was completed when the Two Thousand Guineas and the One Thousand Guineas were run for the first time at Newmarket in 1809 and 1814 respectively.

Meanwhile the very active Jockey Club was taking great strides in making its authority felt in what had been a fairly anarchic and undoubtedly rather villainous racing world. Lord George Bentinck, often called 'The Napoleon of the Turf', followed Sir Charles Bunbury as formidable leader of the Club. Bentinck's father, the Duke of Portland, had won for the Jockey Club the legal right to warn undesirables off Newmarket Heath and his son was active in introducing further innovations. He began the practice of parading the runners in the paddock prior to a race, along with that of numbering the horses. And it was Lord George Bentinck who began the system of starting races with a flag.

Following on Bentinck came another tremendously able 'Dictator of the Turf', Vice-Admiral the Honourable Henry James Rous, who virtually ran racing affairs from the middle of the nineteenth century until his death in 1877. Rous was the ultimate authority on the rules of racing, and in 1850 he published *The Laws and Practice of Horse Racing*, which detailed the history of the development of the Thoroughbred, the rules of racing and his explanation and interpretation of them and the duties of the racecourse officials, along with actual details of a

number of complicated racing cases.

In 1855 Admiral Rous became handicapper to the Jockey Club and was responsible for drawing up the 'Scale of Weight for Age'. His investigations and observations led him to declare that the Thoroughbred had made tremendous improvements as a breed during the previous century, and that the best racehorses of 1750 would have been beaten by the worst runners of 1850. Englishmen could indeed feel proud of the horse that their country had created.

But there was an unpleasant surprise in store for patriotic English racegoers—a decade after Rous had become handicapper the French horse Gladiateur won the English Triple Crown of Two Thousand Guineas, Derby and St Leger. This outstanding horse, which was owned by the son of one of Napoleon's generals, was promptly nicknamed 'The Avenger of Waterloo'!

Racing had started in France, which was to become one of the foremost racing countries in the world, when the French Jockey Club was founded in 1833 by an Englishman living in Paris, Lord Henry Seymour. He was encouraged by Ferdinand Philippe, Duc d'Orleans, the heir to the French throne. In 1837 the French equivalent of England's Derby, known as the Prix du Jockey Club, was run for the first time at the exquisite racecourse of Chantilly. Two decades later racing was started at Longchamp in the Bois de Boulogne—and just inside the entrance gates to the racecourse was

placed a statue of the famous Gladiateur.

Twenty years after Gladiateur had stunned English racing enthusiasts with this sudden sweeping success, one of the greatest Thoroughbreds of all time appeared upon the English racing scene. This was St Simon, by Galopin from St Angela, and bred by Prince Batthyany. The striking colt was bought at the age of two years by the Duke of Portland for 1,600 guineas after the Prince dropped dead at Newmarket just before the race for the Two Thousand Guineas. St Simon had not been entered for either the Derby or the St Leger, and he was not allowed to run in the Two Thousand Guineas of 1884 because his nomination had become void on the death of Prince Batthyany. But St Simon was to prove his great worth as a racehorse anyway!

He ran in ten races, including the Epsom Cup, Goodwood Cup and Ascot Gold Cup, and won them all effortlessly. His trainer Matthew Dawson, who won the Derby with Thormanby, Kingcraft, Silvio, Melton, Ladas and Sir Visto, said of St Simon, 'I have trained only one smashing good horse in my life—St Simon.' Dawson went on to say that 'The extraordinary thing was that St Simon was as good at a furlong as he was at three miles, as distance never seemed to worry him.'

At stud St Simon was a phenomenal success: he headed the list of sires of winners in England for seven consecutive years, 1890 to 1896 inclusive, and again in 1900 and 1901. Ten of his sons and daughters won seventeen English Classics, and in 1900 his progeny won all five of the Classics—Diamond Jubilee won the Triple Crown of Two Thousand Guineas, Derby and St Leger, Winifreda won the One Thousand Guineas and La Roche took the Oaks. During a total of 22 years as a stallion, St Simon sired the winners of 571 races and £553,158.

Meanwhile, breeding theories were proliferating. The basic maxim right from the start had been 'breed the best to the best' and, by and large, this tenet has guided the development of the racehorse ever since. But there was plenty of room for imaginative schemes of all kinds. One of the most famous was formulated by the Australian Bruce Lowe, who, towards the end of the nineteenth century, listed 43 tap-root mares of the breed in numerical order, based on the number of direct descendants of each mare, through the female line, which had won the Derby, the Oaks and the St Leger up to that time. The number One was given to the family whose foundation mare had given rise to the most winners of these three English Classics among her descendants in female line when the system was compiled. Lowe then allotted the number Two to the female family with the second-largest aggregate of winners of the three Classics, and so on down the line.

Modern knowledge of genetics has, however, shown how basically unsound Lowe's theory in fact was, and it hardly ever plays a part nowadays when breeders are working out the matings of their animals.

There were many other theories which captured the interest of Thoroughbred breeders at one time or another. Among them, Friedrich Becker's Theory of Female Influence postulated the conclusion that the factors being handed on in straight male line descent, when intensified by inbreeding, cause the sire line to degenerate, and Colonel J. Vuillier's System of Dosages was based on the analysis

St Simon, pictured here as an old horse, was one of the greatest race horses and sires of all time
Left: the quality features of a top race horse of today, Mill Reef

of a horse's pedigree to the twelfth generation, by which time all of 4,096 ancestors had come under scrutiny! From his work Colonel Vuillier concluded that certain sires were desirable in a balanced 'mixture' in a pedigree to produce a top-class racehorse.

One of the most notable breeders and owners of the twentieth century in Europe, the Aga Khan, was so impressed by Vuillier's theory that he employed the Colonel as his manager and adviser, and certainly the Aga Khan had great success. He bought his first yearling in 1921, and three years later came up with his first Classic winner, Diophon, which captured the Two Thousand Guineas. Altogether, his famous racing colours of green with chocolate hoops were carried to victory in no less than 36 European Classics. These wins included five English Derbies, six St Legers and six Irish Derbies.

The Epsom Derby of 1933, however, fell to the extremely popular English-bred Hyperion, measuring just 15·1½ hands on the day that he won the premier Classic by four lengths. Hyperion, by Gainsborough out of Selene, was bred and owned by the then Lord Derby, and ran in thirteen races, winning nine of them and being placed three times in a career that lasted three years. At two years he was fast enough to win the New Stakes at Royal Ascot, and the same year he took the Derby, he also won the St Leger.

Hyperion went on to become one of the most successful sires of this century. He was the leading sire of winners in England six times, and sired the winners of eleven English Classic races, including Derby winner Owen Tudor. Another of Hyperion's famous sons was Aureole, which won the King George VI and Queen Elizabeth Stakes and the Coronation Cup, was placed second in the Derby, and was leading sire in England in 1960 and 1961. Among Aureole's successful sons are Derby Winner St Paddy, also a sire of note, and Saint Crespin III, winner of the Prix de l'Arc de Triomphe and another successful sire. Hyperion's great influence as a sire was, in fact, felt in just about every racing country in the world, with America no exception. There he sired the stallions Alibhai, Khaled and Heliopolis.

This century has also seen the incredible successes of the Italian breeder Federico Tesio, hailed by many as a genius. He bred two of the greatest racehorses and sires both of this century and of all time, Nearco and Ribot, as well as a host of other outstanding animals.

Nearco, by Pharos out of Nogara, was the unbeaten winner of fourteen races from five furlongs to a mile (1 to 1·6 km), including the testing Grand Prix de Paris. Tesio himself summed up the splendour of the horse he bred, trained and later sold to an English stud by writing, 'Beautifully balanced, of perfect size and great quality. Won all his fourteen races as soon as he was asked. Not a true stayer, though he won up to 3,000 metres. He won these longer races by his superb class and brilliant speed.'

Nearco was twice leading sire of winners in England, and was in the list of the top ten sires for fifteen consecutive years, from 1942–56 inclusive. He was the sire of two Derby winners, and another two Derby winners were from mares by Nearco. Interestingly, he carried four crosses of the fabulous St Simon in the first five generations of his pedigree. The Italian-bred, English-based stallion also had a profound influence on breeding in the United

States; his son Nasrullah was leading sire in England once and in America five times, and is the world's leading sire of Stakes Winners with 101 of them to his credit. Nasrullah's son Bold Ruler, sire of the 'super horse' and 1973 American Triple Crown-winner Secretariat, is the second leading sire of Stakes Winners.

Significantly enough, too, the recent American-bred Epsom Derby winners Sir Ivor, Nijinsky, Mill Reef and Roberto are all male-line descendants of the truly great Nearco.

Federico Tesio's other phenomenal home-bred horse was Ribot, which won all sixteen of his races, including the Prix de l'Arc de Triomphe twice and the King George VI and Queen Elizabeth Stakes. The average winning margin in Ribot's races was six lengths, and when he was retired to stud at the age of four he had won more prize money in Europe than any other single Thoroughbred up to that time.

At stud Ribot had an equally brilliant career; he was leading sire in England in 1963, 1967 and 1968, and in the top five on the lists of leading sires in the USA, France and Italy. More than fifty of his progeny have won high-class races, and they include such famous animals as Ragusa, Ribocco, Ribero, Molvedo, Tom Rolfe, Graustark, Arts and Letters, Long Look, and Romulus.

In Switzerland races are often held over snow, known as the 'white turf'; there is something uniquely exhilarating about them

During recent years Europe has seen some outstanding racehorses; the beautiful Brigadier Gerard was hailed as one of the best horses bred and raced in England in this century as he won seventeen races from eighteen starts, including the Two Thousand Guineas and the King George VI and Queen Elizabeth Stakes; Grundy in 1975 won the Epsom Derby, the Irish Sweeps Derby, the King George VI and Queen Elizabeth Stakes, and the Irish Two Thousand Guineas; and, during the last few years, the American-bred fillies Dahlia and Allez France have added an extra element of lustre and excitement to the European racing scene. Other recent notable performers have been Mill Reef, Nijinsky and Sir Ivor.

America

During the last decade, American Thoroughbred breeding has risen to the top of the international tree, and today the best American bloodstock is the most sought-after in the world. Sir Ivor, Nijinsky, Mill Reef, Roberto, Dahlia, Allez France, San San, Pistol Packer—these are just some of the Thoroughbred stars that have come to Europe from American pastures to win the biggest races that the Old World has to offer.

Why have American racehorses had such resounding success abroad in recent years? American breeders lay a great emphasis on speed in the Thoroughbred, they have purchased the best foreign bloodstock whenever possible, and they rigorously apply the so-called 'racecourse test', meaning that American horses are raced much more often and harder than their counterparts in Europe, and therefore are asked to prove their soundness and toughness to a much greater degree.

Sheer speed has been and still is the great American racing passion. Of the races staged for three-year-olds and over in North America, 56 per cent are held over distances of 6 furlongs (1·2 km) or less, and 80 per cent are run over a mile (1·6 km) or less. But speed is the inverse of stamina, and American breeders found that their racehorses were badly lacking in staying power. They therefore went to the British Isles, France, Italy and South America looking for breeding stock that would rectify this deficiency.

The result today is that there is hardly an American-bred horse of standing which does not contain some imported blood 'close up' in its pedigree. During the 1970 racing season in North America, for instance, 97·3 per cent of American-bred winners of stakes worth $10,000 or more had imported ancestors within the first three generations of their pedigree. And 73·2 per cent had imported blood in the first two generations of their family tree. This obviously means that the best so-called American-bred racehorses are not 'American' in the fullest sense of the word—foaled in America, they are the product of a recent judicious mixing of American and foreign bloodlines. The result is the combination of the scintillating speed that thrills American racegoers plus enough stamina to capture Europe's Classics.

For instance, Never Bend, the sire of the famous American-bred Mill Reef, now standing as a stallion at Britain's National Stud, never won a race of more than nine furlongs (1·8 km). And before the

appearance of his Prix de l'Arc de Triomphe-winning son, Never Bend had not sired an animal which had won a race over more than a mile and a quarter (2 km).

Even more surprising, Traffic, the sire of Rheffic, the 1971 winner of the French Derby (1½ miles or 2·4 km), himself never won a race of more than six and a half furlongs (1·3 km)!

Another contrast between American and European racehorses is the number of times that they compete. Four of the greatest European-bred sires, for example, were St Simon, which raced ten times for ten victories, Hyperion, which ran in thirteen races, Nearco, which was unbeaten in fourteen races, and Ribot, which won all sixteen of his races.

The great American sire Bold Ruler, on the other hand, started all of 33 times for 23 victories, and was unplaced only four times in all these races. Bold Ruler's son Bold Commander, which sired 1970 Kentucky Derby winner Dust Commander, ran in 41 races between the ages of two and four for seven wins and eleven places.

But the racing record of the famous Stymie makes these numbers of starts almost pale into insignificance—before he finally went to stud at six, Stymie had competed in all of 131 races!

The overseas successes of the best American-bred racehorses are directly reflected in terms of demand and prices paid at the select yearlings sales in the United States. At the 1975 Keeneland sale of select yearlings, for instance, foreign buyers, mainly Europeans, spent nearly $4,850,000—more than 26 per cent of the sale gross.

Horse-racing was introduced to America, as was the Thoroughbred itself, by the first British colonists of the Maryland-Virginia 'tidewater country' in the early part of the seventeenth century. America's first horse races were staged in the short main streets of the burgeoning towns—later the race fans chopped narrow quarter-mile-long (400-metre) straight raceways in the woods and held their racing there. Towards the middle and end of the seventeenth century the rich planters of the South began to import some fine racehorses from England, and it was not long before racetracks suitable for them were being constructed. Nevertheless, the first formal racecourse was laid out in the North, at Long Island, New York, and was called Newmarket, in honour of Britain's racing 'headquarters'.

By the time of the American War of Independence there was considerable breeding and racing of horses, and the racing Establishment boasted

The photo-finish has made it possible to establish with certainty just whose nose passes the finishing post first; here both horses and jockeys are giving everything they've got in those last few yards

The state of Kentucky is the heartland of American Thoroughbred breeding. These youngsters live in the famous blue grass region near Lexington Opposite: a class two-year old canters down to the start

George Washington and Thomas Jefferson amongst its members. Once the War was over, racing soon got back into its stride. Between 1784 and 1798 four stallions were imported from England which had considerable success in America and founded highly successful lines. These sires were Medley, a neat, good-looking son of the famous Gimcrack; Shark, by Marske, the latter being the sire of the mighty Eclipse; Messenger, by Mambrino, the foundation stallion of the American Standardbred breed and a successful sire of gallopers as well; and Diomed, mentioned in the section on European racing, which had won the very first running of the Derby at Epsom, and which, after a long, undistinguished stud career in England, was to found an enduring line in America. One of his famous sons was Sir Archy, the greatest racehorse and sire that had been foaled in America up to that time.

American breeders, however, still resorted to England for new importations and brought in some excellent sires. One of the most successful was Glencoe, purchased in 1838, and for eight years the leading sire of winners in America. One of his most notable get was the filly Peytona, who won more races than any member of her sex to that time.

Early on, the gentlemanly South with its big houses, leisured life and tradition of fine horseflesh was the centre of racing and breeding, with Virginia and Maryland leading the way. However, the increasing wealth of the North, particularly New York, led to a growing interest in racing there, and this in turn sparked North-South rivalry in the racing of Thoroughbreds.

The first big clash came in 1823 when William Ransom Johnson, a Southerner, pitted Sir Archy's son Sir Henry against the Northern racer American Eclipse, which belonged to the New Yorker Cornelius van Ranst. American Eclipse won this contest, but in 1836 Johnson got his own back by racing his John Bascombe against the New Yorker's Post Boy. Six years later, though, Johnson got an unpleasant shock when his highly fancied Boston travelled north to be beaten by the New Jersey-bred mare Fashion.

Fashion, too, was defeated in turn, by Peytona in 1845, the last of the great North-South contests before the more serious conflict between North and South began. In the years preceding the American Civil War, racing had become strongly established at racetracks in New York, Baltimore, Chicago, Cincinnati, New Orleans, Charleston and St Louis.

The holocaust of the Civil War meant the end of the old Thoroughbred stud farms of the tidewater country, and Kentucky, which had missed out on much of the wartime devastation and where some of the old Virginia horse breeders had resettled, became increasingly important. Racing, too, had suffered from the hostilities, but as soon as the war finished the sport sprang back to life with a renewed vigour. In 1864, while the Civil War was still in progress, Old Saratoga staged its first meeting, and in the decade after the end of the conflict the major racetracks of Pimlico, at Baltimore, the Fair Grounds at New Orleans, and Churchill Downs at Louisville, were inaugurated. All these racetracks are still functioning today, and Churchill Downs is now the home of the world-famous Kentucky Derby.

Meanwhile, due to the intense pressure of certain religious groups which disapproved of racing and betting, horse racing disappeared from many of the Southern states where it had formerly flourished.

Some time after the end of the Civil War, the Americans introduced the now-universal crouching jockey's seat, at first derided in England as 'the monkey on a stick' seat. Its effectiveness did not take long to be proved, however, with the outstanding American jockeys Tod Sloan and Danny Maher as two of the leaders in this race-riding revolution.

About this time, a number of coloured riders joined the top ranks of American jockeys, the most successful being Isaac 'Ike' Murphy, who won 44 per cent of the races in which he rode. But like England's gifted Fred Archer, he did not live to enjoy the fruits of the considerable sums he had earned, for he died at the early age of 37, soon after he had retired from race-riding.

In the years following the end of the Civil War many of the most important American races were first staged. In fact, the War was still being fought when The Travers, the oldest stakes event in North America, was first held in 1864. The American Triple Crown races came into being not long after: the Belmont in 1867, the Preakness in 1873, and the Kentucky Derby in 1875.

A fast, balanced start can be an important factor in success in races over short distances

Naturally, this upsurge in the popularity of racing meant that a number of really outstanding Thoroughbreds were seen in action: Ruthless, a very fast filly, won the first Belmont Stakes; Norfolk was an unbeaten star; and Longfellow took part in some stirring renewals of the old North-South race-track clashes.

It was during this period, too, that some of the great lines of American Thoroughbreds were firmly established by stallions of the calibre of Hanover, Domino and Ben Brush.

By the close of the nineteenth century racing was flourishing in the United States as never before. Many called it a 'Golden Age' for American racing. But there was another side to it—of fixed races, doped runners, horses racing under names other than their own. The eventual result of these ever-

increasing abuses, and the publicity they attracted when discovered, was a great public outcry against the whole sport. Much repressive anti-racing legislation was enacted, and by 1911 only two States, Maryland and Kentucky, still had horse racing. Many racehorse owners had to ship their animals to Canada or abroad, and American racing was in a perilous state indeed.

Nevertheless, in 1908 in Kentucky the answer to American racing's plight had already been found. It was the brainchild of Matt Winn, who was then running Churchill Downs at Louisville, the home of the Kentucky Derby. The staging of the 1908 Derby had been threatened when a law was passed forbidding the continuation of trackside bookmaking —but Winn had a solution. He installed totalisator machines, brought over from France, which ena-

bled the betting public to establish its own odds according to the various amounts bet on each horse in a race. Winn had, in fact, already tried out the machines on the Churchill Downs public without success, but now that there were no 'bookies' the pari-mutuel machines found instant public favour. The 1908 Kentucky Derby was saved—and so was racing in the United States.

The pari-mutuel machines provided the States with a straightforward way of taxing revenue from racing. When the bookmakers were operating trackside, it had been difficult to levy taxes on racing income, but with the machines giving a complete record of betting, it was obvious to the tax-gatherers that a regular percentage could be deducted from each betting pool in return for licensing racing —thus producing substantial revenues. Not only that, the machines made it more difficult for gamblers to pull off big coups, which had played an important part in bringing the sport of racing into

such public disrepute.

As a result of the introduction of the pari-mutuels and the keen-eyed vigilance of the state racing commissions which were formed to police the sport, racing made a big comeback at major centres. Once again America was able to watch the racetrack exploits of such performers as the Triple Crown winners Sir Barton, Gallant Fox, Omaha, War Admiral, Whirlaway, Count Fleet, Assault and Citation. There was Regret, only filly ever to capture the Kentucky Derby, and Zev, which beat Epsom Derby winner Papyrus in a much-heralded match race at Belmont Park. So many names of so many outstanding horses—Bold Ruler, Swaps, Nashua, Round Table, Native Dancer, Stymie, Tom Fool, Buckpasser, Damascus, Dr Fager, Kelso . . . .

But of them all—and there have been some truly great ones—two horses, both of a burnished chesnut colour, stand clear. They are Man o'War,

The reaching stride of a French filly cantering down to the start. The racing seat enables jockeys to keep their weight well forward at the gallop

fondly nicknamed 'Big Red', and Secretariat.

Man o'War was foaled in 1917 at a stud farm near Lexington, Kentucky. He was by Fair Play out of Mahubah, by Rock Sand, which had won England's Triple Crown in 1903. Sold as a yearling at Saratoga for $5,000, Man o'War had a tremendously successful two-year-old season; out of ten starts he won nine races. In the race which he failed to win by only half a length, the Sanford Memorial, his admirers claimed that his rider had him facing the wrong way at the start!

At the end of Man o'War's two-year-old season, the *Daily Racing Form* handicapper placed him at the top of the American two-year-olds of 1919 with a weight of 136 pounds (16·6 kg)—16 pounds (7·2 kg) above the second animal on the handicap, Blazes. He grew into a massively splendid three-year-old, standing 16·2 hands high and weighing around 1,150 pounds (521·6 kg). He had a broad chest and a great amount of heart room.

Incredibly enough, Man o'War did not race in the Kentucky Derby, because his owner, Samuel D. Riddle, thought that the race asked too much of a three-year-old at the beginning of May. So the colt's first race at the age of three was in the Preakness, and he took this Classic easily by one and a half lengths. He went on to win the Withers Stakes of one mile (1·6 km) in New York in record time, and in the Belmont Stakes he passed the winning post twenty lengths ahead of the only other animal that had remained in the race.

After winning his next race, the Stuyvesant Handicap, Man o'War took part in what many regard as his most famous race: the Dwyer Stakes of nine furlongs, in which 'Big Red' faced John P. Grier, carrying 18 pounds (8·1 kg) less. The two colts raced neck and neck until they turned into the stretch, when John P. Grier's jockey urged on his much smaller mount to surge past the huge Man o'War. As John P. Grier sprinted ahead, Man

o'War's rider, Clarence Kummer, started to use his whip on the big chesnut, which lengthened out his stride in immediate response. Locked together again, the two colts flashed past the mile post in 1 minute 36 seconds, two-fifths of a second ahead of the track record. But the smaller horse had reached its peak, and Man o'War went on to win the race by a length and a half in the new American record time of 1·49¹/₂.

During his almost unbelievable three-year-old career, Man o'War raced eleven times for eleven victories, including, as well as those mentioned above, the Miller Stakes, the Travers, the Lawrence Realization, the Jockey Club Gold Cup and the Potomac Handicap.

Finally, in 1920, Man o'War ran in a match race against Sir Barton, the best three-year-old colt of the previous year, which had won the Kentucky Derby, the Preakness, the Belmont and the Withers. The match race was staged over ten furlongs at Windsor, in Ontario, Canada, and Man o'War won by seven lengths, breaking the track record by 6²/₅ seconds. At the end of 1920, Man o'War's earnings

had reached $249,465, a new American record.

At stud Man o'War also did very well, although many authorities think that because he was virtually a private stallion he did not cover nearly as many good mares as he would have done if he had been at public stud, and so his potential as a sire was never fully exploited. Nevertheless, he was America's leading sire for 1926, and was among the ten top broodmare sires for all of 22 years. He sired the 1937 Triple Crown winner, War Admiral, which in turn was leading American sire in 1945.

Amongst Man o'War's other distinguished progeny were War Relic, Clyde Van Dusen, Bateau, American Flag, Florence Nightingale, Crusader, Edith Cavell, Mars, Annapolis, Battleship and Scapa Flow.

The great Secretariat was foaled more than fifty years after Man o'War, in 1970, at the 2,600-acre (1,052-hectare) Meadow Stud near Doswell, Virginia. He was a splendid-looking foal from the moment of birth, and his breeding was superlative: by the great Bold Ruler out of Somethingroyal, a mare which had already produced Sir Gaylord, a

In many parts of the world races are held over dirt tracks rather than turf—this is over a very wet track at the Aqueduct, New York

111

top racehorse and highly successful sire (he sired the 1968 Epsom Derby winner, Sir Ivor).

Towards the end of his yearling year Secretariat went to veteran trainer Lucien Laurin to prepare for his future on the racetrack. In his first start, at two, the tall chesnut colt was heavily bumped into by another runner at the start of a maiden race, took time to get into his stride, and finished in fourth place.

But next time out Secretariat won a maiden race by six lengths, and then picked up an allowance race at Saratoga. His next contest was the Sanford, in which he defeated another good horse, Linda's Chief. Trainer Laurin's hopes were high, and they were justified as Secretariat swept all before him—the Hopeful by five lengths, the Futurity by two, the Laurel Futurity by eight and the Garden State by three and a half. He also won the Champagne Stakes by two lengths, but had bumped another horse during his drive to victory and was disqualified.

His final tally for his sparkling two-year-old season was seven wins and $456,404 from nine starts.

At three Secretariat quite simply became a legend. He won his first two races, then surprisingly finished only third in the Wood Memorial, held two weeks before the Kentucky Derby.

In the Derby he started slowly and was in last position for the first part of the race. Then he started to move forward—and kept going relentlessly until only Sham was left in front of him as they turned into the home stretch. Secretariat's rider Ron Turcotte flicked down his whip, and the giant chesnut flew past Sham into the lead and on to victory and a new Kentucky Derby record.

In the second leg of the American Triple Crown, the Preakness, Secretariat soon took command and stayed in front to win by two and a half lengths. This time Turcotte never had to move his whip.

Then the Belmont, the last of the Triple Crown races, and, at a mile and a half, the longest. The race was one to remember forever—Secretariat ran the first ten furlongs in an even faster time than he had galloped the record-breaking Kentucky Derby! At the finishing line he was an incredible 31 lengths clear, and he smashed the record for the Belmont by $2^3/_5$ seconds.

Above: a portrait of the Byerley Turk, one of the founding stallions of the English Thoroughbred Left: a famous racehorse, by a famous painter: a portrait of Eclipse by George Stubbs

*Above: the handsome
vivacity of the
Thoroughbred: the
Queen's Albany, with
Jo Mercer up
Right: the field sweeps
around Tattenham
Corner in a recent Derby
Opposite: part of the
scene at an Australian
picnic race meeting*

*A legend in his own time:
the steeplechaser, Arkle
Opposite: a string of
racehorses goes out to
exercise on a frosty
winter morning*

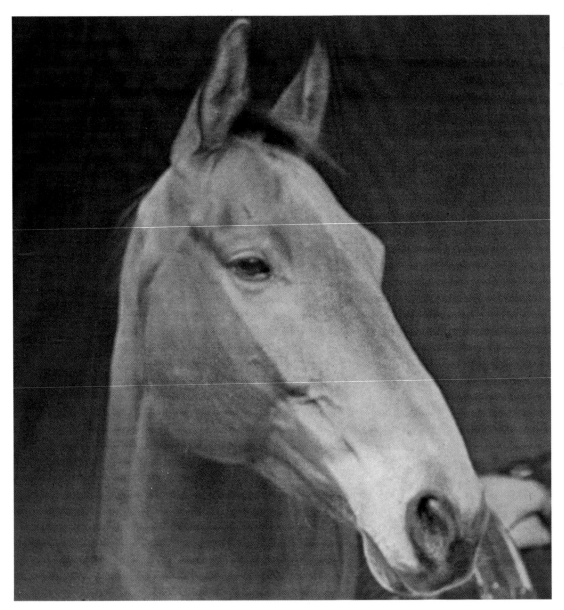

Arkle, who was only once unplaced in seventy races—and won thirty-five of them Below: a point-to-point meeting; competing horses qualify by hunting a certain number of days during the season

*Horse and rider in
beautiful harmony:
Nonoalco canters before
the start of the 1974
Epsom Derby*

*Above: the brilliant
Nijinsky, the winner of
England's Triple Crown
in 1970
Right: a fall over
the solid timber of a
three-day event
cross-country course
Opposite above: over the
last—and a hard battle
ahead as the two leaders
race for the finishing post
Opposite below: an Irish
horse negotiates a drop
fence on the cross-
country course*

Above: the field flows over an obstacle in a hurdle race
Right: the most formidable steeplechase fence: Becher's Brook, on the Aintree Grand National course, where so many horses come to grief
Opposite: a great showjumping combination: Marian Coakes (now Marian Mould) and her outstanding pony, Stroller

Captain Mark Phillips, seen here after winning the Badminton Horse Trials, is one of the world's top three-day event riders
Opposite: the American event rider, Bruce Davidson, peers through the spray at the Munich Olympic Games. Most cross-country courses include daunting water jumps, which are a good test of the horses' obedience

*Anneli Drummond-Hay
and Merely-a-Monarch,
outstanding in both
three-day events and
showjumping competitions
Below : an Australian
event horse surges
boldly through the water
Opposite : the
showjumping phase of a
three-day event :
Princess Anne and
Doublet in excellent
style*

Showjumping and Eventing

Showjumping

Showjumping began as an organized sport around the middle of the nineteenth century. In 1865 the Royal Dublin Society's show staged a jumping contest and the next year there was a jumping competition in Paris, with the contestants first parading indoors and then going outside to jump a course of mainly natural obstacles. Jumping became particularly popular on the Continent, especially in France and Germany, and jumping contests formed part of the Olympic Games of 1900 held in Paris. In 1901 German and Swiss officers went to Turin, Italy, to compete against each other and Italian officers over jumps.

It was in Italy that the great revolution in jumping took place when Caprilli introduced the so-called 'forward seat' over obstacles. Previously, riders had believed that they should lean back, feet stuck forward, and with long reins, when descending, and it did, in fact, take Caprilli and his disciple Santini a long time to prove that the new forward jumping seat was a much more effective and much safer one. It is, of course, universally employed in showjumping today.

Showjumping has gone from strength to strength during the twentieth century, but it really came into its own as an important international spectator sport only after the end of World War II.

Britain has produced many great riders and horses, with Colonel Harry Llewellyn and his famous Foxhunter, Pat Smythe with Prince Hal and Tosca, Peter Robeson and Craven A, and Wilf White and Nizefela as some of the best-remembered combinations from the immediate post-war period.

The very successful All-England Jumping Ground at Hickstead, south of London, was opened in 1960 by Douglas Bunn. The stars of British showjumping have all been seen there, with, among the ladies, the names of Marion Mould, Alison Westwood, Anneli Drummond-Hay and Anne Moore immediately springing to mind. Two of the most famous male riders have been the extraordinary David Broome, who somehow manages to make the most difficult courses look so easy to jump, and the controversial and highly skilled Harvey Smith.

The Continent has also produced its share of great showjumping riders during the last thirty years, with West Germany claiming two of the most famous, Hans Gunter Winkler and Alwin Schockemöhle. Winkler will always be remembered for his performance at the Olympic Games in Stockholm—he had been injured before the final round and was in so much pain that he was hardly able to keep himself in the saddle, yet, relying on his marvellous little mare Halla, he was able to go clear around the huge course and clinch both the Individual Gold Medal and the Team Gold Medal for his country. Schockemöhle, one of the great international showjumping riders of all time, is also one of the most popular of contestants with both spectators and fellow competitors.

Other Continental riders of note have been the d'Inzeo brothers from Italy, Pierre Jonqueres d'Oriola from France, riding Lutteur, Ali Baba and Pomona, and 'Paco' Goyoaga of Spain.

The New World has played its part, too, with Nelson Pessoa from Brazil, and a number of top-notch American riders, headed by the scintillating perfectionist Bill Steinkraus. The United States showjumping team has been consistently successful at the highest level, and much of this success is said

Alwin Schockemöhle, one of Germany's major show jumping competitors jumping at Hickstead

to be due to the superlative training of the team by Bertalan de Nemethy, who became team trainer just before the Stockholm Olympics.

In modern showjumping one of the most important individuals is the course builder; if a course is too easy the contest will be dull, with one clear round after another piling up for a long-drawn-out jump-off against the clock; but if even the best showjumpers in the world are presented with a course which is too big, and in which the distances are too awkward, the result will be an uninspiring shambles. The ideal is to build a course which will

be varied and interesting for competitors and spectators alike, and which will fully test the abilities of the animals taking part, without 'over-facing' them in any way.

In the early days of showjumping, courses were very simple indeed. In Britain, for example, the courses at agricultural shows used to consist of six to eight fences down one side of the ring, a similar number along the other side, and perhaps a triple bar or water jump in the middle. On top of the fences were slats which were easily brushed off. Time was of no importance whatsoever, which meant

that contests often used to drag on interminably.

Nowadays, however, courses are very sophisticated, with much imagination and skill, plus great experience, put into them by the top course builders. That courses are as varied as they are is quite remarkable, since, in fact, only four different types of fence exist: the upright, the parallel, the staircase and the pyramid.

The very first thing a course builder must do is ascertain the class of jumper he is constructing the course for; novice, Grade B or international. When putting together a course for international jumpers,

the course builder will use the size of the fences, the distances between them, the distances between the various elements of a combination fence, and the position in which they are to be placed in relation to one another and also in relation to the perimeter of the ring.

Working on the accepted basis that a horse's stride at a strong canter will be some 10 feet (3 metres), fences which are situated more than 80 feet (24·4 metres) apart are considered to be unrelated, in other words there is enough distance between them for a horse to change its pace and stride.

Captain Raimondo d'Inzeo of Italy, another very well known and successful showjumping rider at the Olympic Games in Mexico in 1968

131

If fences are within 39 feet 4 inches (11·9 metres) of each other they are considered to be part of a combination fence, which is generally formed of two or three elements. It is the distance between fences as well as their height that makes them easy or difficult to jump: for instance, between two uprights an easy distance for one stride would be 26 feet (8 metres), for two strides it would be 35 feet (10·5 metres).

The type of fence also has a fundamental bearing on how well horses will jump it. A really solid-looking obstacle will usually be cleared more often than an upright with three poles, and a triple bar will be easier for the horse than an upright of exactly the same height. A spread of, say, 4 feet (1·2 metres) in width will be more difficult than one that is 8 feet (2·4 metres) wide.

One of the most difficult of all obstacles has always been the water jump. Riders and their mounts seem to get on better with the water jump today than they used to, but it still threatens, and there is always a great collective sigh of relief from the crowd when a popular rider successfully clears the glinting surface of the water. Mistakes seem to

be most often made at the water jump because some riders tend to kick on towards it with a 'fingers crossed' approach. Interestingly enough, if a pole is put over a water jump it will suddenly become one of the easiest obstacles of the course because the need for the horse to gain height will almost always mean that he will achieve the width as well.

Riders put a lot of time and effort into schooling showjumpers on the flat. They need to instil instant obedience into an animal, and to make it as responsive, balanced and supple as possible. This is why leading showjumpers can circle tightly in a balanced, rhythmic canter when asked, can change leads as required, and back easily. The German showjumping riders, with their traditional background of dressage, probably have the most highly schooled mounts of all on the flat, and the many long hours of this sort of training seem to pay off in giving their riding an admirable precision and control.

Naturally, a showjumper does not need to have all the collection of the dressage horse, but it should be able to engage its hind legs properly, have a properly rounded topline and, ideally, an instant responsiveness when asked to speed up, slow down or turn.

Hans Winkler shown (left), demolishing the wall at the Horse of the Year Show, and (right) smoothly negotiating a fence on the Olympic show jumping course at the Mexico Games

David Broome, a truly great British rider, jumping in exemplary style with Manhattan Right: Bill Steinkraus, for many years captain of the United States international show-jumping team, and an Olympic gold medallist

The first step in training a horse is working to get him fit. Outdoor exercise, schooling work, feeding and grooming all play their part. The rider will then work the horse in increasingly difficult movements, suppling and balancing him at the same time as he trains him in reacting to the combined aids of legs, hands, seat and weight. Half-turns on the forehead and on the haunches will make the animal even more responsive to the leg, and he will also be taught to respond to the opening rein, to the neck rein and to the direct rein of opposition.

Many horses will be schooled in the exercise of the shoulder-in, the basic training for all lateral work, which will also help to supple and collect him. Performing the rein-back will increase engagement of the hind legs, and the counter canter will refine the showjumper's response to the aids.

Jumping work is started without a rider on the horse's back. The animal is first lunged over low cavaletti poles, which stand, for work at the trot, about 8 inches (200 mm) high and are separated from each other by one of the horse's normal strides. As schooling over the cavaletti progresses, this distance is gradually increased to lengthen the animal's stride.

Before beginning work over the cavaletti, the trainer will warm up the horse on the lunge so that he will go enthusiastically forward in an active trot.

At first the horse will be asked to trot over just one pole, then another pole will be added, making sure when only two poles are used that more than the distance of a stride separates them. This is done so that the animal will not mistake them for a combination obstacle and attempt to clear them in one long bound.

More cavaletti poles are added one at a time as the horse progresses until there are half a dozen of them. By this time the future showjumper should be freely trotting over them with confidence, rhythm, balance and suppleness. Ridden work over the cavaletti can then be started. All this schooling is performed at a rising trot to prevent too much strain being placed on the horse's back.

Initially, most exercises, whether over cavaletti or small obstacles, are performed at the trot. There is a general rule that a horse will not be asked to do anything with a rider on his back that he has not already done riderless at the end of the lunge rein.

As the trainer begins to make the jumping work on the lunge more demanding, he will introduce the horse to a variety of small fences, all brightly coloured, asking the animal to stretch across wider obstacles before he starts putting him at the upright ones. Many showjumping experts do not like to use a ground-line or guardrail before a fence when training a horse, as they say this practice teaches it

to judge its fences by the bottom rather than by the top, which is a bad habit.

At this stage, with work progressing into a more complex pattern, the trainer will want the horse to use its neck correctly, to raise its shoulders and to stretch properly over a spread. Some horses naturally handle spreads better, others are more capable over uprights—the trainer will have to observe his charge carefully with experienced eyes, and balance the jumping work accordingly in order to develop the animal's weaker points. He will make sure that all poles on uprights are in the same plane and that there are always enough of them to keep the fence from appearing hollow. The best spread fences for beginning showjumpers are low, wide 'oxers', but as they are raised the trainer maintains a constant check to ensure that they do not look too hollow; he also builds them in an ascending line,

since horses will more readily jump this type of spread. A horse that does not stretch out properly over spreads at this stage can be encouraged to do so by placing a pole on the ground at an appropriate distance on the landing side.

A technique that is often used to get a horse going properly before a fence is to precede the obstacle with three or four cavaletti set at a maximum height of 18 inches (457 mm), with the appropriate spacing between them. Once a horse can handle such a basic arrangement effectively, it is time to introduce it to a combination of upright and spread. Usually an upright is followed, after a distance of three strides, by a spread. As the jumper learns to cope well with such a combination, the distance between the obstacles can gradually be reduced to two strides, then to one full stride and, finally, and only when the horse is really ready for it.

Continental European riders, especially those with military training, often have a strong, controlled riding style, and prefer big, strong horses to ride

HRH The Princess Anne, who has done a great deal to popularize combined training events, is a first-class horsewoman. Here she takes Collingwood round the showjumping course at the Crookham Horse trials

down to one very short stride. With this lesson well learned, the position of the fences is reversed and the exercise can then be repeated.

When the horse is going enthusiastically, capably and quietly over obstacles on the end of the lunge rein, it is time to introduce a rider. The first

fences a horse faces with a rider on its back are well below its developed capability, and between obstacles it is brought back to a walk, trotting or cantering only for the last few strides before reaching each fence. This practice not only teaches the horse to 'use' itself to the maximum, but also accustoms it

Harvey Smith, both a controversial and a popular figure in international show jumping, competing at Hickstead with Evan Jones

to the proper control right from the very beginning.

Once this initial schooling work over obstacles has been fully mastered, the rider can start working his mount over a training course. Now the speeds required in actual competition will be practised, and the horse will become used to producing longer or shorter strides as demanded by the rider. Variations of speed at the canter are conscientiously practised, both on the flat and round the training course.

Uprights become higher, spreads wider, and combinations more demanding as the showjumper makes progress. The horse is also taught to jump both spreads and upright fences at an angle—this is done by building obstacles that can be jumped from either side and riding the horse in a figure of eight with the fence at its centre. This lesson also provides quite an exercise in approach and control. At first, the rider makes the loops of the figure of eight so narrow that the horse reaches the fence almost straight, but as the animal progresses the loops are gradually widened, and so the angle of approach widens as well. This schooling exercise is said to cure horses which have a tendency to run out always to the same side: if a horse, for instance, always tends to run out to the right, then work is done approaching the fence from the right so that it is virtually impossible for the horse to escape to that side.

The trainer is now ready to add another vital technique to the showjumper's armoury—he will teach it to turn in the air as it is clearing a fence so that it will land facing in another direction, and so

be able to gain time in a speed competition. If the rider wants to turn right on landing, he will turn the horse's head to the right during the jump, tightening the right rein while allowing with the left, and with the right leg acting behind the girth.

Gradually, the horse is introduced to the more difficult obstacles it is likely to meet in the jumping arena. It will be required to negotiate banks and water jumps, but there should be no great problems as long as the trainer makes sure that these new obstacles are small and that a 'schoolmaster' (an experienced horse) is present during the first few lessons to give a lead to the novice.

Finally, after this period of skilful, concentrated training, the horse will be ready to take part in its first showjumping competition, and from there, hopefully, it will sooner or later work its way into the big time!

Eventing

To the French cavalry goes the honour of initiating the antecedent to the modern three-day event, the *Championnat du Cheval d'Armes*, which was first staged near Paris in 1902. The part of the competition involving dressage was held in a covered riding school, a steeplechase was run over the Vincennes course, a roads and tracks section of 50 kilometres (30 miles) across country, and the showjumping was at the Grand Palais in Paris. This first *Championnat du Cheval d'Armes* was extremely successful,

Anneli Drummond-Hay was a champion three-day event rider before devoting her time to show jumping

The fences on the cross-country course are big, solid and often formidable, like this obstacle in a German competition

and was repeated annually from then onwards.

Sweden soon followed the French lead, staging a military three-day event for the first time in 1907 at the Stronsholm cavalry school. Belgium's cavalry officers took up the sport three years later, and the Swiss military followed suit in 1921. Next to take up the demanding equestrian event was the cavalry of the United States.

The sport belonged to the cavalry officers from its inception right up until the outbreak of World War II, and was generally known, appropriately enough, as the 'Military'. The winning horse was supposed to represent the ideal cavalry charger —bold but calm, well-schooled for parade, agile, supple and instantly responsive in battle, untiring on long marches, a good jumper, and of a sound, robust constitution so that it could go on giving of its best for days on end. Such a horse also pre-supposed a courageous and skilled rider.

After the end of the Second World War, how-

ever, the scene had altered radically. The days of mounted cavalry in the field had gone forever, and the sport of combined training became the province of civilian riders and their mounts. Britain had played a minor role in pre-World War II eventing, but after the War British riders and their horses were to become some of the very best in the world.

The *Fédération Equestre Internationale* (FEI) describes the three-day event as 'the most complete combined competition, demanding of the rider considerable knowledge in all branches of equitation and a precise knowledge of his horse's ability, and of the horse a degree of general competence resulting from intelligent and rational training.'

The FEI further defines the objects of the contest as demonstrating 'the rider's spirit, boldness, perfect knowledge of his horse's paces and their use across country' and 'the condition, handiness, courage, jumping ability, stamina and speed of the well-trained horse.'

A three-day event is constituted in the following way: the first day is devoted to dressage, the second day to speed and endurance tests, and the third and final day to showjumping.

The dressage test, which lasts about ten minutes only, consists of the performance of a series of connected movements on the flat, all of which should be linked smoothly together and performed as correctly and with as much style as possible. Dressage is the more advanced training of the horse on the flat, and transforms him into an instantly obedient, balanced, supple and graceful animal. The riding of the dressage test calls for great precision on the part of the rider, who must direct his horse from one marker in the dressage arena to another with the lightest aids possible, and who should blend with his mount to give the impression

that horse and man are acting as one unit. Of considerable importance in this test are the so-called 'translations' from one pace to another or from one speed to another, such as walk to trot and back to walk again, or from a longer-striding to a shorter-striding trot, with the appropriate alteration of the horse's outline.

The three-day event dressage test consists of some twenty movements, carried out from point to point within the low railings of an arena measuring 60 metres (65 yards) long by 20 metres (22 yards) wide. The movements include changes of direction and circles at walk, trot and canter, the paces being sometimes collected and sometimes extended, with many testing transitions. The horse must halt easily and stand squarely, waiting attentively for his rider's next command, which may well be the one to

For three-day events you need a bold and willing horse: Lucinda Prior-Palmer has brought out these qualities in Be Fair

141

rein-back for a few steps. It will also perform sideways movements.

The dressage test is watched throughout by three experienced and eagle-eyed judges, each of whom marks every movement out of a total of 6. The judges also award marks for the general impression given by the horse during the performance. Their markings are pooled and an average is taken. The reason for this is that the appreciation of dressage is, by its very nature, somewhat subjective, and the judges' individual preferences for a certain type of horse or style of riding may mean that the marks they award differ considerably.

The second day's testing of speed and endurance is divided into four phases, each of which is timed independently. The horses set off individually, separated by intervals of 5 minutes. Phases A and C, which can consist of between 6 and 12 miles (9·7 and 19·3 km) along roads and tracks, are ridden easily, at trot and canter. Phase B, though, is all go—some twelve fences of a 2 to 2½ miles (3·2 to 4 km) steeplechase course which must be ridden at a fast gallop. Phase D, the cross-country, consists of riding 3½ to 5 miles (5·6 to 8 km) over open country at a good gallop and jumping some thirty fixed, solid and often rather frightening-looking obstacles. A scale of penalties is applied to the time taken for each of the phases, with falls or refusals being heavily penalized.

The second day of a three-day event calls for boldness, strength and stamina on the part of the horses, and courage, decision, determination, judgment and much skill from the riders. Both horse and rider must be really fit for the second day—the steeple-chase course must be ridden fast, not wasting a second, and the obstacles they face in the cross-country phase are not for the even slightly faint-hearted. Judgment of pace is also at a premium in this part of the contest: if a rider goes too slowly over the steeplechase course he will lose marks, and if he pushes his horse along too fast he will tire the animal unnecessarily. Over the cross-country course the rider must get the horse going in a good rhythm and jumping in his stride, since if they approach the obstacles too fast the horse can easily become unbalanced.

The final day of the competition is devoted to jumping a simple and fairly small course in a normal showjumping arena. To eyes used to the top showjumpers, the obstacles at a three-day event look almost puny, but the fact is that many of the horses will have been severely tested by their efforts of the previous day and will be quite tired and perhaps even rather stiff.

If riders are separated by only a few points at the start of the jumping test, it will be an exciting finale with much pressure on the riders. It is obviously a time for a cool head, steady nerves and some very positive thinking! And it can show who, in the final analysis, are the true competitors.

While three-day events are the star occasions of the combined training world, they are far outnumbered by one- and two-day horse trials, which are modified versions of the three-day event. One- and two-day trials consist of the same three main tests, modified to suit the occasion. The dressage test is shorter and easier, and marked by one or two judges. The cross-country is the equivalent of Phase D, but is not as long and has fewer obstacles, and the jumping takes place over a smaller course with

fewer fences for the horse to clear.

In one-day horse trials the jumping is often held after the dressage test which opens the competition. In two-day horse trials a few miles of roads and tracks and a short steeplechase course are included.

The regulations for international and Olympic three-day events are laid down by the FEI, and the championship structure follows that of many sports —there are World Championships midway between Olympic Games, and Continental Championships in the year following one Olympic Games and in the year preceding the next.

In these competitions the different nations draw for the order of starting, a rider from each team being sent off in the order drawn. The team captains may decide in what order their team members are to ride, with four members per team being the usual complement. The final team classification is worked out on the basis of the scores of the three best-performing riders. Teams of three riders are also allowed, but then all three scores must count.

Training for this totally amateur sport is a long-drawn-out, time-consuming business, and it requires a great deal of dedication. Many British riders will begin training for the eventing season soon after the New Year. The first objective is to get the horse fit, and to this end a great deal of steady walking is done. As the horse starts to harden, the rider will begin trotting him and then will go on to work at the canter. Once the animal is in good condition, serious work in dressage and jumping will begin, with plenty of practice in galloping across country. Many riders are anxious to get their mounts ready for the first horse trials in March.

These early trials play a large part in furthering the event horse's training: by taking part in them he becomes familiar with the conditions of competition, is made fitter, and his courage and ability are tempered in the heat of contest. Many riders school their horses over quite small cross-country obstacles at home, restricting the animals' experience of bigger ones to the actual trials. In the horse trials held in the early part of the year, riders like to take

A popular sort of obstacle with course-builders, and a difficult one to jump comfortably

On the way down: falls are inevitable, but fortunately there are very few really serious accidents

their horses to straightforward, galloping courses where the animals can stride out freely and without too much checking and turning, and where, consequently, they will really enjoy themselves. This helps greatly in building up and maintaining their enthusiasm, which is an important factor in the much more testing conditions of the big three-day events staged later in the year.

If horse and rider form a top combination which wins at, say, a famous three-day event like Badminton in April, then it is probable that they will be short-listed for the team which will contest the Championships in the autumn. The horse would be turned out for a few weeks to rest and to benefit from the spring grazing. Towards the end of May or the beginning of June it will be brought in once more, and the sort of training schedule detailed above would begin all over again, with success in the Championships as the goal!

Ponies

The most appealing of all equines, for many people, are undoubtedly the ponies. Ranging in size and type from the tiny Shetland to the sleek British Riding Pony, their charm and gaiety—not to forget the winning wilfulness they can often display—endear them to children, adolescents and adults alike.

The world's most elegant pony is the Riding Pony of Britain, which combines the alert, engaging personality and the basic characteristics of the pony with the refinement and sweeping action of the best type of Thoroughbred. In the years following the end of World War I breeders began to develop the Riding Pony as a definite show-ring type. There was a great upsurge of interest in the 1930s, and as a result many excellent Riding Ponies were to be seen at Olympia in the years preceding World War II. These gems of the show ring had evolved as a result of crossing small Thoroughbred polo pony stallions with mares of British Native Pony type, mainly the Welsh.

Pony breeders were able to use these small Thoroughbred stallions towards the end of the 1920s—this was when the height limit for polo ponies was raised, and as a result many of the small Thoroughbred stallions which had been used for siring the smaller polo ponies were no longer needed. The Native Pony mares they were mated with were sound and courageous, with iron-hard constitutions. As the Riding Pony began to take shape as a type, there was also an addition of Arabian blood to include a touch of special elegance in the animal's make-up.

Many modern authorities believe that the Riding Ponies nearest to a fixed type are to be found in the 13·2 hands high class. They say that the animals in the 12·2 hands high class often tend too much towards Native Pony type, while those in the 14·2 hands high class can often look like miniature horses rather than ponies.

The superb result of an inspired crossing of Thoroughbred, Welsh and Arabian was seen in the most famous Riding Pony stallion of all time, Bwlch Valentino, the sire said to be responsible for introducing the characteristic sweeping action of today's Riding Ponies. Valentino's dam Goldflake was by a Thoroughbred, Meteoric, whose sire Sunstar won the Derby and the Two Thousand Guineas. Goldflake's dam, Cigarette, was a 13 hands high Welsh-Thoroughbred cross which had been an outstanding racing pony in Wales. Goldflake did well in the show ring before World War II, and as an old mare of nineteen she was sent to the 15 hands high polo pony sire Valentine, by the Thoroughbred Malice from the Arabian mare Silverspray. The result was the legendary Bwlch Valentino, which went on to found a dynasty of Riding Pony stallions.

One criticism levelled at Riding Ponies is that they are often too 'hot' in temperament for most children to ride. The pony's knowledgeable admirers refute this assertion, however, claiming that a Riding Pony's temperament is largely a matter of how it is broken in, ridden and treated generally. They do say, nevertheless, that the Riding Pony is not an animal for a beginner.

Britain is extremely fortunate in possessing a plethora of Native Pony breeds, one of them dating from prehistoric times. Some of the best known of these Native Ponies are the Welsh—the sturdy yet refined, Welsh Mountain Pony is particularly popular.

The Welsh Mountain Pony does not exceed 12 hands in height, and should be hardy and spirited.

A Welsh Mountain pony, with elegance and power in the animated movement typical of this breed

It can have any colour except piebald or skewbald. Its head is characteristic and very attractive— small, clean-cut, well-set and tapering to the muzzle, with large bold eyes and well-placed, small pointed ears. Its nostrils should be prominent and open, and its jaw and throat should be clean and finely cut, with ample room at the angle of the jaw. The Welsh Mountain Pony's neck should be lengthy, well-carried, and moderately lean in the case of mares; stallions, though, should have rather 'cresty' necks. The shoulders should be long and sloping well back, the withers should be moderately fine, and the humerus should be upright so that the foreleg is not set in under the body.

The pony's forelegs should be set square and true, with long, strong forearms, well-developed knees, short, flat bone below the knees, pasterns of proportionate slope and length, and round, well-shaped, dense hoofs. The girth should be deep and

the ribs should be well sprung, while the back and loins should be muscular, strong and well coupled. The hindquarters should be lengthy and fine, with the tail well set and carried gaily. The hind legs should not be too bent, and the hocks should be large, flat and clean with prominent points, and turn neither in nor out. Also, the hock should not be set behind a line from the point of the quarter to the fetlock joint.

One of the most important aspects of the Welsh Mountain Pony is its action, which is very carefully judged in show classes, and which should be quick, free and straight from the shoulder, and well away in front. The hocks should be well flexed in movement, with straight and powerful leverage, and they should travel well under the body.

As well as being very pleasing to the eye, the Welsh Mountain Pony is also a truly tough character. It has always been bred on the Welsh hills, with-

out pampering, and is the inheritor of a very hardy constitution and a very alert nature. Its attractive movement is also the result of centuries of living in rough country, where it is sure-footed, quick and full of action.

The so-called 'Section B' Welsh Pony (which occupies Section B of the Welsh Pony and Cob Society Stud Book) must not exceed 13·2 hands in height. Section Bs have many of the characteristics of the Section A Mountain Pony, but are bred as children's riding ponies, and the tendency is for them to be finer in type—although the purists insist that they should be of the same type as the Section A Welsh ponies, but larger, and with more emphasis on their riding qualities.

Another extremely attractive 'Welshman' is the Welsh Pony of Cob type. This active, high-stepping pony does not exceed 13·2 hands in height, and evolved by blending Cob blood with pony blood. The head should always have a definite pony look with no hint of coarseness, and it should possess presence and zest in abundance.

Finally, there is the Welsh Cob, for which there is no height limit, although most are between 14·2 and 15·1 hands high. They should be compact and strong, never common, with plenty of bone and plenty of presence. The Welsh Cob should be very active and have very good balance.

Britain's oldest Native Pony breed is the Exmoor, which lived in the Exmoor area of present-

Crickhowell village, with its ancient bridge over the river Usk, makes a tranquil background for this Welsh mare and her foal

A herd of Exmoor ponies roam with their foals in their native north Devon Opposite, above: A Dartmoor pony mare, well protected against the weather by her thick coat, with her young foal Opposite, below: A delightful New Forest foal, also well wrapped up against the cold. The quality of New Forest stock has been greatly improved in recent years

day Devon and Somerset in prehistoric times. Theirs has been a tough environment for many centuries, and so those Exmoor Ponies which survived to propagate the breed were especially hardy and wily. They are exceptionally strong for their size, and a sturdy Exmoor Pony of some 12 hands will find no difficulty in carrying a robust grown man.

Exmoor Ponies should not be taller than 12·2 hands, although stallions of up to 12·3 hands may be permitted. They are bay, brown or mouse-dun in colour, with characteristic mealy muzzles, and are lighter in colour inside their thighs and on their bellies. They should have wide foreheads, large eyes and wide-opening nostrils, and their chests should

be deep and wide. The loins should be powerful, the legs clean and the feet hard.

A neighbour of the Exmoor is the Dartmoor, which is also tough and hardy, and is noted as a jumper. Dartmoors have played, and continue to play, an important role in the breeding of larger all-round ponies. Dartmoor Ponies are strong, well made and good looking, with small, well-bred heads. They have strong shoulders, backs and loins, and full manes and tails. It is said that the good front and fairly high head carriage of the Dartmoor makes him seem especially safe to child riders.

The New Forest Pony roams the woods and heath of that large wild area in Hampshire. Ponies

of the breed have been living in the New Forest since the eleventh century, and over the hundreds of years the original blood has been mingled with the bloodlines of other ponies and even horses. The result is that there are now considerable variations in type in the New Forest Pony, whose size ranges from 12 to 14 hands in height. The larger ponies are good all-rounders and learn quickly. The best type of New Forest Pony should have a handsome head, a good length of rein, a short back, and strong loins and quarters. The legs should have plenty of bone and be well-muscled on forearm and gaskin. Most New Forest Ponies are still running free in the Forest, but their breeding is overseen to some extent nowadays in that the stallions are inspected every year and only those which meet the Breed Society's high standards are allowed to reproduce.

Highland Ponies are strong, attractive small ponies which come from the Highlands of Scotland.

The breed used to be divided into two types, mainland and island. The mainland ponies stand about 14·2 hands high, while the island type is sometimes no more than 12·2 hands in height. The Highland is very strong and exceedingly sure-footed, and was often used as a pack animal. Even today, many a Highland Pony earns his keep carrying deer carcasses down the steep slopes of his native land. Highland Ponies have deep and powerful bodies, with broad chests. Their heads are neat, with large, kind eyes, and their legs are short and very robust, with much bone. Most of them are a shade of dun, which can range from gold-brown to silver blue, and may have a dark dorsal 'eel stripe'.

Another Northerner is the far-famed miniscule Shetland, which comes from the islands of Shetland and Orkney, off Scotland's north coast. It is only some 10·2 hands high, and, despite its smallness, is very strong, being, in fact, the strongest of all Native Ponies for its size. It has a small, refined and most attractive head, an abundant mane and tail, and, in winter, a very thick coat. The Shetland has a lot of character, and can often possess a most independent turn of mind.

The Fell Pony of Northern England is native to Cumberland and Westmorland. It is descended from the Celtic pony, and had a long and important history as a pack animal, being used to carry lead from the inland mines to the ports of the North East. The Fell has a strong, compact body, strong, squarely set legs and round, open, hard feet. Its head is prick-eared and attractive, and it carries its tail gaily. Not over 14 hands high, Fell Ponies are usually black, dark brown or bay in colour. In the past, Fells were used as trotters and for general farm work as well as pack animals. Nowadays, they are used mainly for riding, and some still earn their living in remote areas as shepherd's mounts.

A similar type of pony to the Fell is the Dales, which originally came from the same basic breeding

stock. It is found mainly in County Durham and Northumberland. The Dales is the largest Native Pony, and also the strongest of them. As it is capable of carrying a heavy man all day across rough country, it has found much modern employment as a trekking pony. Formerly, Dales Ponies were used for general farm work. They cross well with the right sort of Thoroughbred to produce excellent hunters.

From Ireland comes the Connemara Pony, which is said to be descended, at least in part, from animals imported from Spain in those remote centuries before the Romans arrived in Britain. In fact, the Connemara does have a rather Andalusian-looking head and its general conformation is in many ways similar to that of the Andalusian. Connemara Ponies are grey, brown, black, bay and dun in colour, with the occasional roan or chesnut. The Connemara Stud Book was started in 1923, and is restricted to animals of more than two years of age which have been approved by an Inspection Committee. In Ireland the ponies must be 13·2 to 14 hands high, but in England they are allowed to go up to 14·2 hands in height. Conformation-wise, the Connemara should be deep-bodied and well ribbed-out, with a good sloping shoulder, well-balanced head and neck, and short strong legs. They cross well with Thoroughbreds and Arabians.

Probably the best-known pony from the Conti-

nent is the Haflinger, which comes from the South
Tyrol area of Austria. The breed was created by the

mating of Arabian stallions with local mares, and
this Arabian involvement is shown by the refined

head of the Haflinger. The ponies are always chesnut with flaxen manes and tails, their colour varying from a very dark liver chesnut to a pale golden colour. They are very robust and strong, with equable temperaments, and are used by the farmers of their native mountain country. There is considerable variation in type, with some individuals being built as real work animals, while others are lighter and with more scope, and therefore more of riding type. In height they range from 12·3 hands to 14·2 hands, with a height of 13·3 hands being held as the ideal.

The breeding of the Haflinger is a very interesting example of complete State control, a control which is reputed to have made an enormous improvement in the breed in only a quarter of a century. Individual breeders are allowed to own only mares, not stallions. All colt foals are carefully looked over by government officers at weaning, and only about a score are passed out of three or four hundred. These selected few are taken to the government stud farm. They are inspected again at three years of age, and those which pass this second rigorous test are permitted to stand as stallions.

Haflinger mares must also gain official approval before being permitted to breed. They are inspected as weanlings, then as yearlings. And at three comes the most searching examination of all: government inspectors make a final decisions on the basis of the fillies' height, girth, bone measurement, colour, conformation, temperament and action.

In France's picturesque and swampy Camargue lives a white pony that, although not very attractive in appearance, is extremely functional in its native surroundings. Standing no more than 14 hands high, the Camargue pony has a rather large, plain head, a short neck, straight shoulders, a good back and strong loins, and a sloping croup. It is used as a mount by the *gardians*, the black-sombreroed cowboys of the Camargue, to herd their black and savage fighting cattle. The Camargue Pony is very strong for its size, very agile and surprisingly speedy. It also possesses a great knowledge of the terrain, which seems to come very close to instinct, and in the rush-covered land of treacherous quicksands and sudden deep channels the Camargue Pony can be trusted to keep its less perceptive rider out of trouble.

The elegant, chestnut mountain pony of the Tyrol, the Haflinger, photographed against an impressive Austrian background
Opposite : Welsh Mountain Ponies are probably the most beautiful ponies in the world—but they are also very tough and hardy

153

Above: the cowboys of France, the gardians, *riding their tough Camargue ponies through that region's marshy country*
Below: a spotted pony. Ponies carrying spots are very popular in North America

Another well-known European pony is the Fjord from Norway. These dun ponies are said to spring from an ancient breed which was indigenous to Norway, and which roamed there even before Viking times. Still other theories place the Fjord Pony as a direct descendant of the Asiatic wild horse, commonly known as Przewalski's Horse. Today the strong, hardy, good-natured Fjord is very

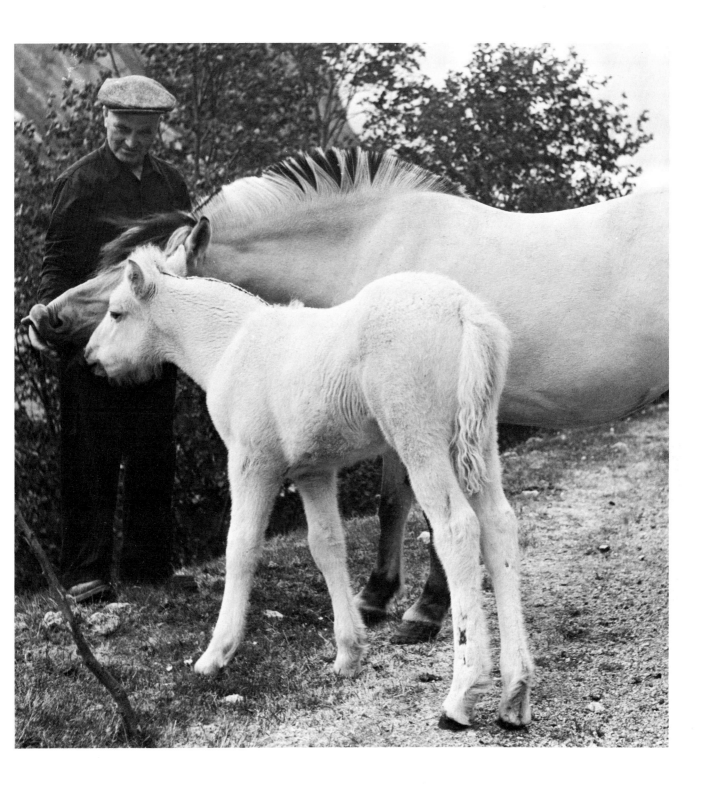

popular as a riding and harness pony in many European countries, and has even been exported as far afield as the United States and Canada. The Fjord Pony stands from 13·1 to 14·1 hands high, and is very long-lived, fertile and frugal, as well as being a very willing worker.

North America has produced one of the most spectacular ponies of the world in its spotted Pony of the Americas. This is a fast, agile and even-tempered miniature version of the Appaloosa, and the association which regulates and promotes the breed is very active in staging all sorts of Western-style competitions and activities for the ponies' young riders. There are even special short races for the unusually marked Ponies of the Americas.

North America is also the home of a number of other pony breeds, drawn from various parts of the world, including the tiny Falabella from Argentina. Interestingly enough, some of the imported breeds bear only a passing resemblance to their cousins in their native lands. The Shetland Pony in America, for instance, is a very refined, high-stepping and high-headed harness pony!

Australia is the home of many of the British

A Norwegian Fjord pony mare, showing the characteristic striped mane of this ancient breed, with her endearingly fluffy foal

breeds of Native Pony, with the Welsh Mountain Pony, the Shetland and the Connemara being particularly popular. There is also an Australian Pony, of fairly recent development, which has its own stud book. Australian Ponies have been developed from blending some of the British breeds, and probably carry Timor Pony blood, from the ponies bred on the island of Timor in the Indian Ocean, as well. They are attractive ponies to look at, and are good-tempered and agile.

Pony Clubs and Riding Clubs

In many parts of the world pony clubs provide a wealth of pleasure and education for the young people who belong to them. In Britain, the Pony Club was founded in 1929 when a branch of the British Institute of the Horse was turned into an organization to create enthusiasm for riding amongst children, and to teach them how to ride and care for their animals correctly. The project was almost immediately successful, and by the mid-1930s there were more than 8,000 members.

World War II put an end to pony clubbing, however, and it was with some misgivings, considering the great interest in things mechanical, that the Pony Club movement was started up again in 1945.

However, there was more interest in ponies and riding amongst young people than ever before, and Pony Club membership is now heading towards the 100,000 figure.

The basis of the pony club is the working rally, and rallies are usually staged in the Easter and Summer holidays. However, in a very cold country like Canada, where there are many enthusiastic pony club members, some of the branches which have a heated indoor school at their disposal hold their Club rallies during the bitter winter months.

The main objective at a rally is instruction in riding and jumping at the appropriate levels, and in the management and care of ponies and their tack. Logically enough, the youngsters attending the rally are grouped in 'rides' according to their level of proficiency. There are rides for all, from the greenest novice to the most accomplished. And along with the serious business of instruction goes plenty of fun and relaxation, plus the sort of worthwhile companionship that can form the basis of firm friendships. There are mounted games, and rides across the countryside, during which the riders can learn country lore, part of the curriculum, at first hand. Such a cross-country ride in Canada can offer a very picturesque scene, since some of the Canadian pony clubs ride Western-style.

Most of the pony club officials provide their

services free of cost. They are kept busy teaching and examining for the various tests, and also training riders for teams which take part in inter-branch competitions. Their instruction is often of the most practical kind possible, with to-the-point advice about bits and saddles and other items of tack. They will also assist members who have problems with their mounts, although they reserve the right to send away any animal that appears to constitute a danger to its own or any other rider. They do not permit the use at pony clubs of mares in foal or with foals at foot, or those ponies which are too old, too weak or too young.

It is not, in fact, necessary to own a pony to belong to a pony club. Many ponies taking part in rallies are hired, and where ponies are in short supply, rides will be taken in turn so that one pony is at the service of two riders. Dismounted rallies are also held, when instruction and demonstration in such arts as feeding or shoeing are given, and visits are made to stud farms and other equine and equestrian establishments.

Eventing is a popular sport that is catered for by pony clubs in many countries. It also provides the mechanism by which pony club members can visit other branches in their own countries and abroad. The South African pony clubs, for instance, have staged the Inter-Territorial Horse Trials, with teams from Britain and Rhodesia. British pony club teams have competed in the United States and Denmark, among other countries, while the Inter-Pacific Exchange brings together teams from Australia, New Zealand, Japan, Canada, the United States and Britain.

In Britain a very special event is the Pony Club Mounted Games Championship, for which the much-coveted trophy is the Prince Philip Challenge Cup. Teams first meet in area competitions, then the winners of these contests vie with one another in the finals which form part of the Horse of the Year Show in the autumn.

One of the brightest spots of the pony club year in any part of the world is the camp. Some of the camps are truly exotic, such as Canadian expeditions to the Rockies, Kenya pony clubs' mounted safaris, and Australian rides into the bushland of the Outback. However, even in less adventurous settings there is a special delight in camping out under canvas, with the ponies tethered in lines cavalry-fashion.

The main activities of a pony club will vary depending on the area. Clubs in heavily-populated, built-up areas may have to do all their work within a covered riding school; many Irish pony clubs are very interested in the traditional Irish equestrian sport of fox hunting; those in affluent districts often have a greater interest in eventing because of the better class of pony available to members.

In Britain most members of pony clubs are actually mounted on ponies. But in America members mostly ride horses, even if some of them are Quarter Horses and Arabians that would qualify as ponies height-wise in the British Isles. The expressed aim of the members of the American clubs is very well worth quoting and remembering: 'To be thoroughly happy, comfortable horsemen, riding across natural country with complete confidence and perfect balance, on a mount that is equally happy and free from pain or bewilderment.'

In Australia, pony club members ride animals

of all sizes, from small round ponies to tall, rangy Thoroughbreds, passing by way of Australian Stockhorses, Arabians, Quarter Horses and their crosses. In the widespread land Down Under the pony clubs vary considerably in interest and attitudes. Close to conservative Melbourne, for example, members are smartly turned out British-style, and are very interested in eventing and show-jumping. There the Inter-Branch Horse Trials Championship is spread over two days, with up to 50 teams taking part. And in fox-hunting Victoria, both the Melbourne and Oaklands Hunts hold special meets for young people. In less sophisticated parts of Australia, however, the pony club members will often be youngsters who have grown up on horseback and who sit in the deep stock saddles of the Australian bush country. Their sun-tanned faces will be shaded by broad-brimmed hats which manage to stay on no matter how fast the rider is moving, and they will probably wear blue jeans. One of the very special occasions for many Australian pony clubs is the 'trek', when members of the club ride from station property to station property, spending a night or two on each of them.

Pony clubbing began in New Zealand in 1944 when the Heretaunga Pony Club was founded. The New Zealand Pony Clubs Association now has more than 80 branches with over 8,000 members. At first the teaching of dressage-style training and riding met with some resistance from those with a background of having 'taught themselves' to ride. How-

ever, it soon became apparent that Pony Club members who paid attention to modern schooling and riding methods were winning most of the gymkhana events, and it did not take long for most of the 'diehards' to follow their example.

In America, the place of pony clubs has largely been taken by the riding clubs, mounted on horses rather than ponies. It is not unusual for as many as several hundred members attired in cowboy clothes to meet together to ride for up to two weeks at a time through the most picturesque countryside of the Western States.

One of the most famous groups is the Desert Caballeros, who set out from Wickenburg, Arizona, each spring to ride through the Arizona desert. The long file of riders winds across country that is straight out of a Western film, riding between huge cacti and rock outcroppings, and often looking out over the eye-stretching expanse of wasteland to the hazy blue mountains in the distance. Camps are made at various strategically placed scenic spots, and one day is devoted to a 'layover', when the Desert Caballeros vie with each other in friendly competitions such as an impromptu rodeo, clay

pigeon shooting, and mule racing.

Southern California stages the husband-and-wife ride known as Amantes y Caballos—literally 'Lovers and Horses' in Spanish. Instead of trekking from place to place, setting up campsites as they proceed, the Amantes y Caballos riders camp for three days in the one spot, and ride the surrounding trails.

A number of American universities have very active riding clubs. Fairly representative of them is the Equestrian Club of Washington State University. It was formed in 1966 to give students a chance to ride and to learn about horses and their management, and it was an immediate success. The Club doubled its initial membership during the first year, and now has well over a hundred members. University staff and students do not have to be horse-owners to belong—the one requirement for membership is a sincere interest in horses and horsemanship.

The Washington State University Club has three teams which provide members with the opportunity to have fun and improve their riding at the same time: the drill team, the horse show team,

Through the stark grandeur of Arizona riders pick their way carefully down a valley slope
Opposite, above: American riding club members and their horses, equipped in Western style, enjoying a forest ride
Opposite, below: A young Australian rider tightens his girth at a Pony Club meeting

and the rodeo team. The tests to see which riders will win places on the teams are held in spring, but Club members start getting ready for the elimination trials long before that. During the tail-end of winter they work out hard in the University gymnasiums so that they will be really fit physically. This is necessary because in the very cold winters of the State of Washington the opportunities for riding are often limited, since the club does not have an indoor school at its disposal.

Washington State University staged its first rodeo in 1969, hosting competitors from about sixteen colleges and universities. The Club's drill team opened each of the four performances of the rodeo. Members of the team wear cowboy hats, leather chaps and vests, and their mounts carry breastplates and nosebands with the University colours of crimson and gray.

The Club's horse show team is busy at shows in the spring, taking part in a variety of events including so-called 'English', Western and breed classes. The members riding in the various teams are allowed to use their own horses, or, if they are not horse-owners, they may use horses belonging to the University which are used in its physical education courses. The social side of the Club is not neglected, either, and at least once a month there is a get-together in the form of a hay ride, a barbecue or a square dance.

Riding clubs in Germany own lavish indoor schools complete with restaurants and bars, and members can keep their horses in the club stables at cost, which is considerably lower than they would have to pay at a commercial livery establishment.

In Spain, membership of a riding club can provide even more luxurious facilities, and some of the equestrian divisions of Spanish country clubs have some of the very best riding complexes, including some of the most splendid jumping courses, that any horseman could ever wish for.

The riding club movement is very strong in Britain, with the various clubs being affiliated to the British Horse Society. When riding clubs were first formed, a certain number of people in the British horse world tended to look upon their members as purely 'weekend riders'. However, while most riding club members are people who earn their living away from horses, and who ride purely for relaxation as often as their busy lives allow, by no means all riding club members are novices. In fact, membership ranges from beginners to professionals, with the welcome mat out for anyone who wants to ride and who has a genuine interest in horses and horsemanship.

Instructional classes and rides are usually held one or two evenings a week, often at a local riding school. Competitions are held at weekends, with many members hiring mounts from riding schools for club events. There are dressage and showjumping contests, and the Riding Club Horse Trials. There are championships for all three of these activities, with area eliminations being staged as a lead-up to the finals held in the autumn at a special Riding Clubs' Weekend. Apart from the various competitions, there are also a number of riding club tests, with appropriate awards for those who pass.

A gypsy pony—though
decidedly scruffy, this
one is obviously a popular
member of the family
Opposite : ponies
gratefully munch their
hay ration on a sharp
winter's day

162

A Welsh Mountain
pony with her foal in the
Black Mountains
Opposite: a charming
palomino pony and foal

165

*A hardy New Forest
pony foal makes its first
attempts to get to its feet
Opposite : pony
weanlings at a sale*

Two pretty foals greet each other on Dartmoor Below: the winsome Shetland pony is the smallest of Britain's Native Ponies

Pony trekking is a good way to explore the countryside and has enabled many people to ride for the first time

High up in the Dolomites graze a group of Haflinger ponies, a native Austrian breed Opposite: a palomino pony waiting at a paddock gate

The Shetland's thick coat helps to protect it from the harsh winters of its native islands Right: a splendid Connemara pony, a native of Ireland Opposite: blacksmiths are a vital part of the world of horses, though today they have become increasingly hard to find

174

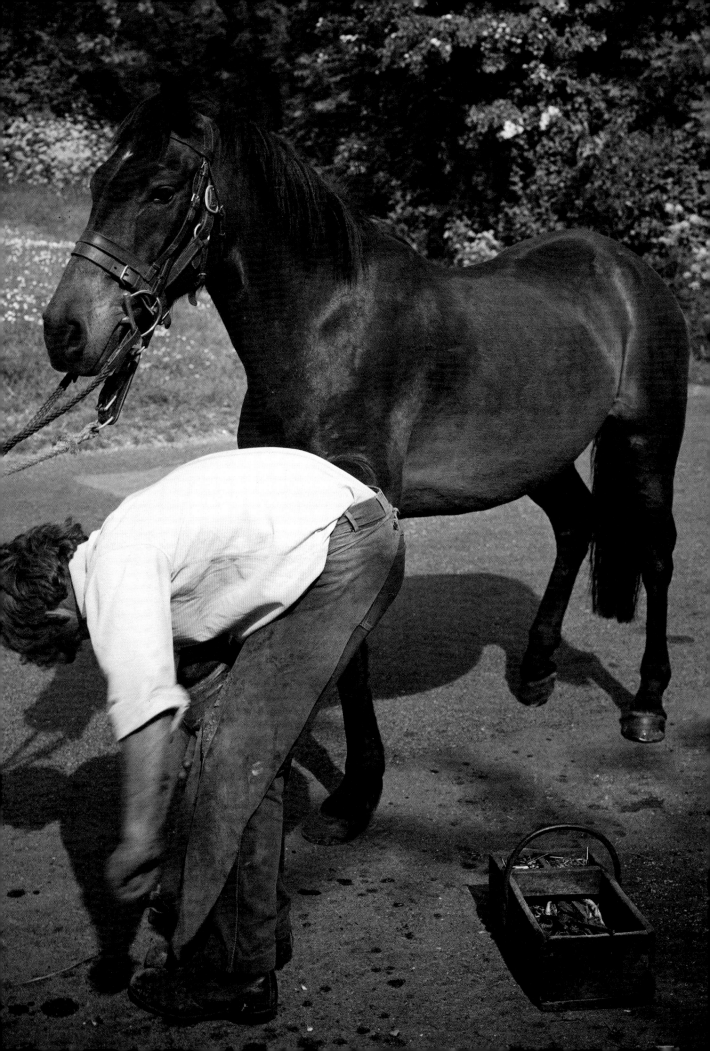

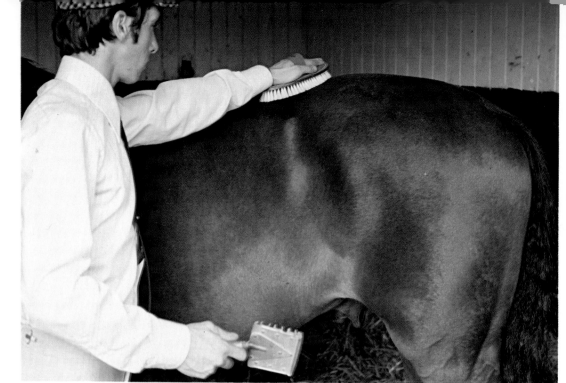

Constant care is needed
for a quality stabled
horse; this photograph
shows the correct way to
use the body brush

A young blacksmith at
work. His job requires
skill, experience and a
good deal of patience as
well as a liking for
animals

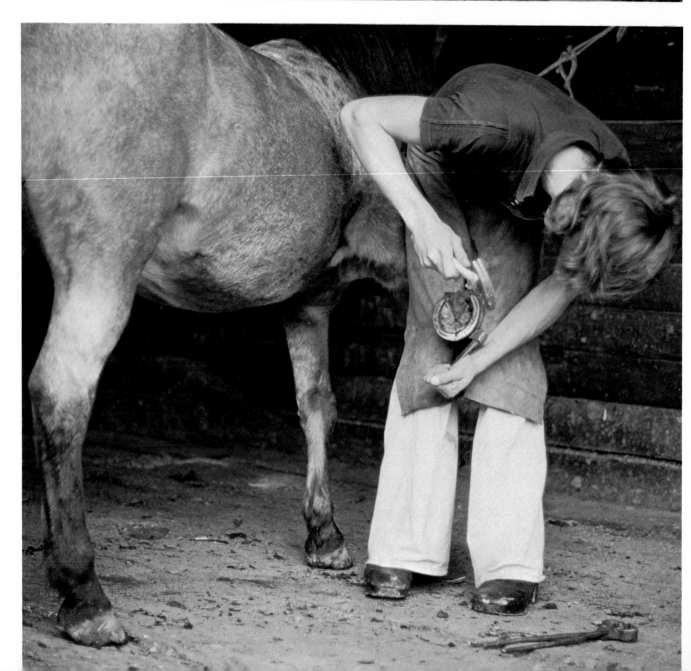

Care and Training

Looking after your own pony or horse so that it remains healthy and happy, good to look at, and perfectly fit for the task that it is required to perform can be one of life's larger satisfactions. But, like any truly worthwhile satisfaction, it is one that has to be earned—in this case by the acquisition of the necessary knowledge followed up by hard work and dedication. For the true horse-lover, however, even the hard work involved can often be pure pleasure.

Ponies, particularly Native Ponies such as the Welsh, Dartmoor or Exmoor, are usually much easier to care for than are horses. Many lightly worked Native Ponies, or ponies carrying a large proportion of Native Pony blood, can live outside all year round, and will require supplementary feeding with hay and perhaps some nuts or cubes only in the late autumn and winter.

First let us look at the sort of paddock that would be required for keeping a pony or ponies. The plural is mentioned deliberately, because one of the most important factors in keeping a pony happy and healthy is that it should have suitable company in the form of one or more ponies of about the same size and type. 'Suitable' means that geldings should run with other geldings and never with mares, and that barren mares should never be turned in with in-foal mares or mares that have foals at foot. The paddock itself should be large enough, with proper fences and shelter that the ponies can use if they want to. There should also be a source of constant fresh water.

A well-drained paddock of about 3 to 4 acres (about 1·5 hectares) in extent is a reasonable size for several ponies on a year-round basis. The grass should be of fairly good quality, ideally of the type found in old-established pastureland, and must not contain any poisonous plants. The most common poisonous plants are the yellow-flowered ragwort, which should be pulled up when seen and taken right away from the animals, allowed to dry out and then burned, most buttercups (which horses will eat if the pasture is poor), foxglove, black briony and monkshood.

Hedges often make the best fences, since they not only contain the animals, but provide windbreaks and shelter in bad weather, and can prevent the ponies in one field from seeing those in the adjoining enclosure. They will require trimming every so often, however, and periodically you should go round looking for any holes which may have developed and block them off with timber (never with wire!).

Post and rails fences are next best to good hedges, but they are expensive to erect. An excellent fence can be provided at far less cost by stretching heavy gauge plain wire between strong posts with the lowest strand not less than 1 foot (300 mm) from the ground. Barbed wire should *never* be used.

If there is no natural shelter in the paddock, it should be provided by means of an open field shelter with its back to the prevailing winds. Ponies will use such a shelter both in winter and in summer—in winter to stay dry and out of the biting winds; in summer to gain relief from the flies which pester them when they are in direct sunlight.

Finally, the paddock must contain a constant supply of fresh, clean water. This can be provided by a running stream, a trough with an automatic filling device or a tank which is kept topped up with fresh water. It is essential to closely inspect the water supply when you take your daily look at the animals, since birds can topple into water containers and drown, automatic filling devices can jam

and either cause an overflow or provide no water at all, and in winter you will often have to break ice on the surface of the water in a trough or tank and scoop it out.

Now let us look at the sort of management which will be required during the various seasons of the year. Management of lightly worked ponies in high summer and early autumn is the easiest of all: no supplementary feeding will usually be required, and you will simply have to check on the ponies and their water supply at least once daily. As the goodness goes out of the grass towards the end of autumn, you may have to start feeding hay, remembering to put it out in more well-separated small piles than there are ponies, thus avoiding any fighting over the fodder. You will probably have to continue to feed hay daily during the winter, and, depending on the severity of the weather and the condition of the animals, you may have to feed nuts or cubes in metal bins. This type of feeding may have to continue until early spring.

With the spring flush of grass will come what is probably the most testing time in the management of ponies. Greedy ponies tend to voraciously consume far more of the lush spring grass than they need—and over-grazing such fresh, highly nutritious herbage can easily cause the foot condition called laminitis. This is an acute inflammation within the outer protective casing of the hoof

affecting the sensitive laminae, and it can cause great pain—so much so, that a pony with a bad case of laminitis will be loath to move a single step, and will remain in one spot as if rooted to the ground.

Therefore, when the first green spring grass is seen, you need to be extra-vigilant and make sure that your ponies do not get too much of it. Keep a close eye on their bodily condition, and if a pony starts to get too fat you will need to restrict its grazing. If you have a field shelter or a loose box, you can keep the pony there during the day with a little hay to prevent it from becoming bored, and turn it out at night to graze. And if it still continues to put on weight, then you must allow it to graze just a few hours each day, or, perhaps, restrict him to a piece of ground that looks really bare. Most fat ponies will find sufficient feed on such a seemingly bare area in spring to keep themselves in good heart.

If a pony should become fat during the early part of the year, it must be conditioned for work under saddle by being exercised at the walk and fairly slow trot, and it should not be asked to go at faster paces until it is obviously much fitter. To bring a fat pony off grass and gallop it is a disaster course!

Ponies and horses require food for three main purposes: to maintain body temperature; to build up and maintain body condition; and to supply the energy needed for movement and for the body's vital

processes. If the weather is cold and the animal is not getting enough food, the first two requirements will take most of the nutrition at the expense of the last one. And if a pony or horse is worked too hard for the amount of food that he is receiving, its body condition will begin to suffer. Therefore, the amount and type of food must be geared to the use of the animal, and this is where eagle-eyed attention to its bodily condition is essential.

Energy is produced by food such as oats and other concentrates. But energy feeds are not natural to the delicate and very special digestive system of ponies and horses, which needs much bulk and roughage. We should not forget that they both developed as wide-ranging grazing animals. In the case of the hard-worked pony in summer, grass will provide all the essential roughage it needs. It will require energy feed too, yet oats would probably make it too 'hot'. The answer is to restrict grazing to a reasonable level, and to supplement this with the correct amount of nuts or cubes and bran. Three pounds (1·4 kg) of nuts daily, mixed with 1 pound (450 grams) of bran and a double handful of chaff, and fed damped, should be sufficient to provide the requisite energy for a hard-working 13 hands high pony. However, it all depends on the individual animal—some will need more, some less.

One point to be noted most carefully at this stage is that you should never feed a pony or horse with cuttings from the lawnmower, since these heat up very rapidly and can easily cause severe colic.

Finally, make sure that the pony gets its required mineral intake by providing it with a mineral block or a large lump of rock salt.

Worm control is another vital facet of pony and horse management. Red worms are the main enemy, and they are always present in ponies and horses and the pastures they graze. Much can be done to cut down worm infestation by a system of rotational grazing, resting the fields regularly and letting cattle graze on them after the ponies or horses have been moved out. Horses are very selective grazers, leaving large clumps of unpalatable grass standing while they concentrate on the same grazed-down patches, and cattle will soon consume the grass that the ponies and horses have left ungrazed. In the process they will destroy many of the worm larvae on the grass, since the larvae cannot live in cattle. However, management of this kind is obviously for the larger establishment, and it would be impractical to suggest it to those maintaining a few ponies on a fairly small area. The best thing to do in this case is to pick up droppings as often as possible, since it is in the droppings that the worm eggs gain access to the pasture, and to dose the animals regularly with anthelmintics (worm medicines).

There are quite a number of different types of anthelmintic on sale, and, since their effectiveness will depend upon a number of factors, it is best to ask your own veterinary surgeon for his advice on this important matter. He will probably make an egg count from a sample of your animal's dung, then advise on the anthelmintic to use and on the

Ponies let out to graze in the evening after feeding

Ponies drinking at a self-filling water trough

strength and frequency of dosage.

Do not take the red worm menace lightly —heavy infestation by these pernicious parasites can cause anaemia, substantial loss of condition, and, in very severe cases, even death.

As winter approaches, the pony will start to grow its thick winter coat, which will provide a natural protection against the rain and cold of the winter months. Virtually waterproof protection is provided by a layer of grease next to the skin, and therefore you must not thoroughly groom a pony which is living out during the winter. Restrict grooming to brushing over fairly lightly with a dandy brush in order to knock off the worst of the mud the pony will pick up.

There is an old saying 'no foot, no horse', and it is equally true to say 'no foot, no pony'—so you will need to pay close attention to a pony's feet. If you ride your pony on soft going only, it may not be necessary to have it shod, but its hooves will still have to be trimmed regularly, say every month to five weeks. However, most ridden ponies will need shoeing if they are not to develop sore feet on hard roads and tracks. Every four weeks the shoes will have to be removed, the hooves trimmed, and then the shoes replaced either with the old set, if they are not very worn, or with a new set.

If your pony carries much Thoroughbred or Arabian blood it will probably be necessary to start stabling it at night once the wet cold weather begins in autumn. This is because such ponies usually have much thinner winter coats than the British Native

Breeds. Stabling an animal at night is going to involve you in a lot more work, of course, since you will have to feed it hay in a haynet while it is inside, keep its water container filled, and muck out the box or shed every day after it has been turned out. Perhaps the pony can live out during winter protected by a waterproof New Zealand-type rug, but this will also mean extra work and attention.

Horses are generally worked much harder than ponies, and because of this most of them are stabled and require considerable attention all the time. With regard to stabling, a loose box is much preferable to a stall, in which a horse is tied up in a narrow space facing a wall for most of the day. The bigger the loose box is, the better, and an excellent size for a big horse is one 14 feet by 12 feet (4·3 metres by 3·6 metres). However, most prefabricated loose boxes are no larger than 12 feet by 12 feet (3·6 metres by 3·6 metres), and seem to be effective enough. It is most important for the ceiling of the box to be as high as possible, since the higher it is the more air the horse will have—12 feet (3·6 metres) eaves height is a good height.

Loose box doors are divided into upper and lower sections, and open outwards so that access to the box will not be denied by straw jamming against the lower door or by a horse which is lying across the entrance. The bottom door must be high enough so that the horse will not consider jumping out over it, yet low enough so that the animal can put its head out without having to stretch his neck up uncomfortably. Four and a half feet (1·4 metres) is a

This horse is eating hay suspended in a haynet from the wall over his manger

good height for the bottom door, which should also be at least 4 feet (1·2 metres) wide. If a door is any narrower than this there is a very real danger that a horse will knock its hips and cause considerable damage to itself in a vital and vulnerable area.

Ideally, boxes should be sited on higher ground where there is no risk of flooding in very wet weather, facing away from the prevailing winds and so that they get the maximum amount of sunshine available. It will also help the psychological well-being of the horse if it can see a great deal of what is going on around it when it looks out over the door.

Three other vital factors in stabling are ventilation, drainage and insulation. Ventilation will be perfectly adequate as long as the top door of the box is left open, but it is essential to ensure that there are no draughts, which are as bad for horses as they are for humans. If the top door has to be shut temporarily for any reason, adequate ventilation can be provided with a window of the kind that swings inward from the base so that air enters in an upward direction and not directly on to the animal. It is essential for all windows to be protected by a grille. Louvres set high in one wall of a box are also very useful for ventilation purposes, as they allow rising warm, used air to escape.

Drainage is closely connected with ventilation, since the fewer waste products that remain in the box, the cleaner the air will be. One of the best forms of drainage is to have a slightly sloping concrete floor and an open drainage channel outside the stable door. Many loose boxes do not have any drainage system at all, though, and this does not matter as long as the horse's bedding is properly mucked out daily. It is worth noting, however, that during winter many knowledgeable horse-owners employ the deep litter system of bedding, in which droppings are removed but the wet straw is allowed to remain and is covered with plenty of fresh dry straw as required. The complete bed is removed every so often. People who use the deep litter system say that as well as cutting down considerably on the amount of labour and straw required, it also keeps animals extra warm during the cold season of the year. However, under this system it is essential to have the top door of the loose box open most of the time, and it should not be employed to any extent during the warmer periods of the year.

In Europe, the floors of most loose boxes, with or without built-in drainage, are made of concrete, but in many other parts of the world floors of hard-packed earth are to be found. These are not so good from the drainage point of view, but they provide more warmth and insulation than concrete and are said to be safer for the horses if they manage to scrape aside their bedding.

Wheat straw is the preferred bedding material in many countries, but boxes are also bedded down with peat moss, sawdust and wood shavings. In some very warm, dry places sand is sometimes used as a very effective bedding material, but care must be taken that it is river sand that does not contain salt, since salty sand from the beach is often eaten by horses which will then suffer from sand colic.

181

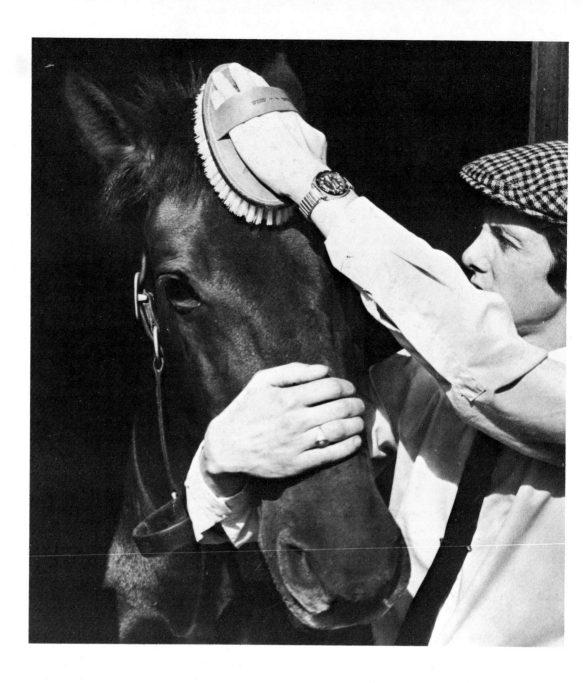

This horse's forelock is being groomed with a body brush

Insulation is the third basic factor to consider, and building materials should be employed in the construction of a box which will keep it cool in summer and warm in winter. Wooden buildings should be properly lined inside, and corrugated iron should never be used as a roofing material for stables, since it attracts heat and does not keep out the cold.

Within a loose box there should be only a minimum of essential equipment: a water manger in one corner, perhaps a manger for feed in another (although many people prefer to feed from the ground in a bin which can be taken out and thoroughly cleaned after every meal), a ring set into one wall for tying up, another for a haynet, and overhead a light that is out of reach of the horse. Light switches, incidentally should be placed outside the loose box where the horse cannot get at them.

Mangers should always be built into the cor-

ners of the loose box at the horse's breast height. They should be gently rounded and never have any sharp projecting points. A water manger can be topped up from a bucket as needed, or can have an automatic filling mechanism. It is essential that both feed and water mangers should be kept scrupulously clean at all times.

Hayracks are undesirable: if they are too high, seeds and dust will drop into the eyes of animals feeding from them; if too low, there is a great danger that horses will get their legs caught up. Either use a haynet tied to a ring in the wall at a height that will prevent a horse from getting a foreleg caught in the net, or simply shake out the hay into a pile in one corner of the loose box. This last system is not as economical as using a haynet, but is much more natural, with the horse feeding from the ground.

One of the cardinal rules of feeding stabled

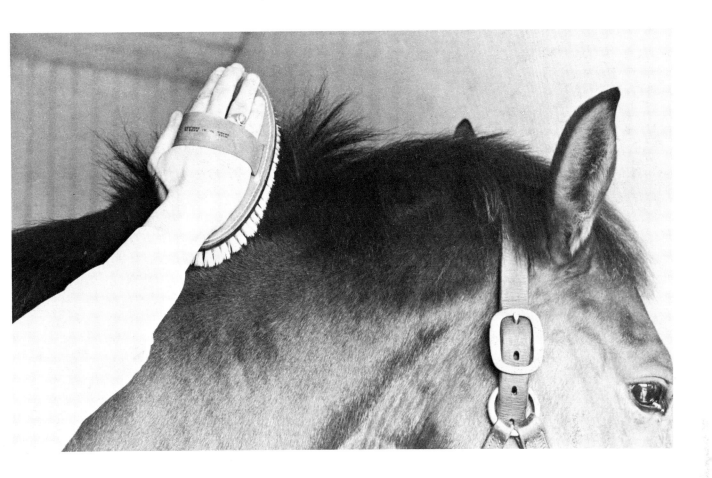

horses is that they should be fed *little and often*. This is because of the very special digestive system of the horse, with its small stomach, which evolved to deal with food taken slowly and almost continuously over extended periods of time. Another cardinal rule of feeding is that a horse should never be worked immediately after a meal. The stomach is located

behind the diaphragm, which is a section of muscle separating it from the chest cavity. In front of the diaphragm are the lungs, and behind it are stomach and liver. Immediately following a feed, the stomach becomes distended and pressure is exerted on the lungs through the diaphragm. This is of no significance when the horse is at rest, but if it were to be worked hard in this condition its breathing would suffer, and the digestive processes would be disturbed. Then it could easily suffer an attack of painful and possibly fatal colic, or the lungs could even choke with blood or the stomach could rupture.

Ideally, a stabled horse should be fed five times a day at adequately spaced intervals, with hay in-between-times; but, if necessary, the number of feeds can be reduced to three. Bulk, energy and auxiliary feeds will be required to provide the necessary amounts of carbohydrates, fats, protein, vitamins and minerals. In many parts of the world, bulk is supplied mainly by hay, which contains a high amount of fibre, as well as protein, calcium and Vitamins A and D. Good hay is greenish in colour, smells sweet, and is springy when a bale is opened. Hay should never be fed, incidentally, in the same year that it was cut. In dry countries where hay is hardly ever grown, such as Spain, Morocco and the Middle East, bulk is most usually provided by chopped straw.

Energy foods consist mainly of oats, barley,

This horse's mane is being brushed with a body brush
Left: a tail-combing session

maize, beans and peas, all of which contain a high proportion of carbohydrates and fats to provide the necessary heating and energizing elements in the horses diet. Oats are preferred when available, since this is the grain most easily assimilated by the horse's digestive system and oats are also highly nutritious. Whole oats should be dry, plump and hard when purchased, and musty or mildewed oats should be immediately rejected. However, oats are often bought crushed (this is done to make them easier to digest) and it is then somewhat harder to judge their quality, although must and mildew will always be apparent.

Among the auxiliary foods are bran, which is the ground husk of the wheat grain and contains a considerable amount of phosphorus, linseed, which is a fattening food, and so-called 'green food' such as carrots, turnips, mangolds, swedes, etc., which aid digestion and add much-appreciated variety to a horse's diet.

Bran is not only nutritious—fed damp it has a valuable laxative effect, and acts in the opposite way when fed dry. Bran mashes are given once a week to

stabled horses in many countries to keep their digestive tracts in good order. Boiling water is poured on the bran (3 pounds (1·4 kg) per horse), a handful of salt per animal is added, the mixture is stirred well, and then left covered (to keep in the steam) for some 20 to 30 minutes.

Linseed contains a high proportion of oil and also a considerable amount of protein. It is absolutely essential to prepare it properly before feeding, since otherwise it can produce the deadly prussic acid inside the horse's stomach. The only way to be sure that this will not happen is to soak the linseed overnight, boil it vigorously for 15 minutes, and then continue to let it simmer for another 6 hours. A half a pound to a pound (225 to 450 grams) of the resultant linseed 'jelly' can then be fed to each horse daily, depending on the time of the year and the condition of the animal.

Incidentally, when feeding carrots, they should be sliced lengthwise, not across, to ensure that they

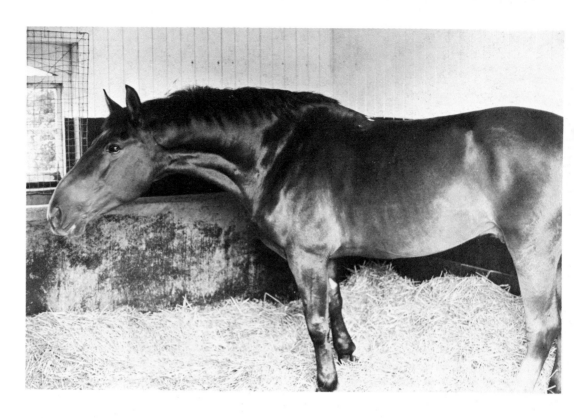

do not block the horse's narrow gullet.

Finally, there are also the various brands of vitamin and mineral supplements, about which you should ask advice from your veterinary surgeon.

The great art in feeding, after making sure that you have acquired good-quality feedingstuffs, is to make sure that a horse's ration is properly balanced for the function it is to fulfil. This is where cultivating an eye for condition will be most helpful, since, while nutritional science can give us basic guidelines about horse-feeding, in the final analysis it will all depend on the individual horse and just how it utilizes the feed with which it is provided.

As a general guide, a horse of about 16 hands in height will require some 4 pounds (1·8 kg) of oats, 2 pounds (900 grams) of nuts, 2 pounds (900 grams) of bran, 1 pound (450 grams) of carrots and 18 pounds (8·2 kg) of hay a day when you first start to condition it. By the time it is really fit and working hard, it may well be receiving 10 pounds (4·5 kg) of oats, 3 pounds (1·4 kg) of nuts, 2 pounds (900 grams) of bran, 1 pound (450 grams) of carrots and 11 pounds (4·9 kg) of hay daily.

Horses in lighter work should receive more bulk food and less energy food, while animals in fast work, such as racehorses, need more energy food and considerably less bulk, although the amount of bulk should never drop below one-third of the total intake, since the horse's digestive system just cannot handle a lot of energy food unless the requisite amount of bulk is also there. Again, it must be emphasized that every stabled horse should be fed as an individual.

A considerable amount of research work has been done in the United States on the nutrition of horses, and animal scientists have come up with some findings which provide sound basic guidelines for practical horse-feeding. They have found that the average energy needs of a 1,000 pounds (502 kg) mature horse for body maintenance (this is before any energy demands for work) are 6·8 pounds (2·9 kg) of total digestible nutrients (TDN). Most types of hay average around 50 per cent in their content of TDN, and therefore such a horse would need some 14 pounds (6·3 kg) of hay for maintenance. Many grains average around 75 per cent TDN, and so a ration of 4 pounds (1·8 kg) of grain (containing 3 pounds (1·4 kg) of TDN) and 8 pounds (3·6 kg) of hay (4 pounds (1·8 kg) TDN) would also satisfy the energy maintenance requirements for this horse.

The animal needs, in addition to TDN for energy, the other main nutrients—protein, minerals and vitamins. The protein requirement for maintaining a 1,000 pound (502 kg) horse was put by the US researchers at six-tenths of a pound (270 grams) of digestible protein or about nine-tenths of a pound (410 grams) of crude protein daily. If the horse were fed the 14 pounds (6·3 kg) of hay mentioned above, it would contain some 1·68 pounds (750 grams) of crude protein, since average mixed grass-legume hay has some 12 per cent crude protein. The ration composed of 8 pounds (3·6 kg) of hay and 4 pounds (1·8 kg) of grain would contain some 1·36 pounds (600 grams) of crude protein, since concentrates contain on average some 10 per cent crude protein. Certainly, either ration would more than take care

of the horse's basic protein needs.

The main minerals required are salt, calcium and phosphorus. Salt should be provided in the manger in the form of a block of rock salt. Hay will usually have quite a lot of calcium, especially if it contains clover or alfalfa. It is often fairly low in phosphorus, which is found in fair amounts in concentrates, which are low in calcium. Therefore, a combination of hay and grain will tend to complement each other in this respect, and provide the correct ration of calcium to phosphorus. Finally, the horse can get its Vitamin A from good-quality, green leafy hay, and its Vitamin D from sunlight and from good-quality sun-cured hay.

Good, sensible feeding must be linked with regular exercise and conscientious grooming. Exercise builds and strengthens the working muscles,

toughens the tendons and sinews of the limbs, and gets lungs and circulation working well. Grooming not only keeps the animal clean, but assists in attaining good condition by toning the muscles and stimulating the skin. The best time to groom a stabled horse, incidentally, is after it has come in from morning exercise.

If a horse is fat when you begin to condition it, you will need to start out with very gentle exercise. And if the horse is too thin, you will have to build it up first with the correct feeding before doing much with it. With horses, going slowly is often the fastest way in the long run—and this old adage certainly applies to getting a horse fit. The amount of exercise must be built up gradually over a time span of many weeks, and it should always contain plenty of variety to maintain the horse's interest and alertness.

Loose boxes at Crabbet Park, Worth, near Crawley, Sussex

An initial period on the lunge, walking and trotting steadily, is a good way to start getting a horse fit. Then there should be a lot of good, steady, long-striding walking under saddle, if possible going up and down a lot of long gradual gradients. Next trotting can begin, and a good, steady, rhythmic trot without any rushing is best. Slow trotting up fairly

gentle slopes helps to improve the wind, and riding over uneven ground will help to develop the horse's balance.

For the first few weeks after work under saddle commences, the horse should generally be exercised for about an hour a day, with about 20 minutes walking and trotting on the lunge to start with,

followed by some 40 minutes mainly walking under saddle, but with a little trotting. By the third or fourth week you can increase the total exercise time to about an hour and a half a day, commencing with 15 minutes on the lunge, some 30 minutes of school work on the flat, and the remaining 45 minutes can be spent gently riding out, preferably over open country where you can ride undisturbed.

By the end of the second month the exercise period can be increased to two hours, with about an hour and a half of hacking, including some steady cantering and the occasional short gallop. Some ten weeks after the conditioning programme was begun the horse should be fit, and then you will have to

On the lunge rein, the horse trots over the pole and one cavaletto Below: still on the lunge, he trots over a series of four cavaletti

Now, with a rider astride, the horse clears a series of four cavaletti

continue to exercise it regularly to ensure that it stays that way.

As mentioned above, grooming is an important aid in the process of getting a horse fit. In grooming, the dandy brush is used to take off any mud, but, because it is stiff and hard, it should never be used on tender parts of the horse's body. Some particularly ticklish horses cannot stand it being used on *any* part of them. The body brush has soft bristles and is for use on the body and legs, and also for brushing out the mane and tail. The dandy brush, incidentally, should never be used on the mane or tail as it soon splits the hairs and pulls them out. Other essential items in any grooming kit are the metal curry comb, which is used to clean the body brush every so often and *never* the horse, the water brush, stable rubber (which is a soft cloth), mane comb and hoof pick.

In winter, stabled horses which are required to work have their heavy winter coats clipped. A long, thick winter coat would soon cause a hard-working horse to sweat, and it would start to lose condition as

a consequence. The lost warmth of the natural winter coat can be replaced by rugs whenever this is necessary.

There are several methods of clipping: a full clip takes off the entire coat, while the hunter clip leaves a saddle patch on the back and thick hair on the legs. This extra protection helps to shield a fine-skinned horse from galls or scalding in the saddle area, and also from cuts and cracked heels on the legs.

Management of a working horse during summer will depend on the activity for which it is used: for instance, an animal ridden out for light hacking could be stabled during the day and turned out at night. Such a horse would probably require very little extra feed apart from some hay to keep it amused while it is inside during the day, and a small amount of concentrate. A hard-working horse, on the other hand, would have to be kept in all the time and fed well. You might be able to turn it out for an hour or so a day in a paddock, however, if it is an animal that settles quietly to graze.

ACKNOWLEDGMENTS

The publishers thank the following sources for photographs:
Black and White: ADN Zentralbild 15; American Hist. Picture Library 38 top l, 104; American Paint Horse Assoc. 38 top r; Australian News and Inf. Bureau 158 top; Austrian Nat. Tourist Office 80; Barnaby's Picture Library 39, 44, 101 top l, 106, 148, 151 top, 154 below, 156, 158 below, 184 top; Camera Press 9 below l, 47, 77, 154 above; John Carnemolla 66 below, 67–71; J. Allan Cash 66 top, 144, 147, 152, 155; Rex Coleman 134 top l; Courtauld Inst. of Art 13 below; Gerry Cranham 78, 98, 100, 105, 108, 110, 111; Anne Cumbers 151 below; ENA 41; Mary Evans Picture Library 40, 73; Keystone Press Agency 76; E. D. Lacey 102, 130–133, 134 top r, 136–139, 141; Leslie Lane 157; M. B. Linney 7 below l and r; Mansell Collection 74, 75, 99; Picturepoint 153; Press Assoc. 109; John Rigby 178–183, 184 below, 185–190; W. W. Rouch 101 top r; John Slater 7 top; Spectrum 8, 12–13, 45, 46, 48, 149; Sport and General Press Agency 10, 107; Sally Anne Thompson 9 top, 11, 18, 19, 33–36, 42–43, 143, 146, 150; Elisabeth Weiland 14, 16, 17, 79, 80, 103, 135, 140, 142.

Colour: Appaloosa Horse Club Inc USA 58; Assoc. Freelance Artists Ltd 166; Australian News and Inf. Bureau 84; Douglass Baglin 64; Barnaby's Picture Library 85; Bavaria Verlag 94, 170; John Carnemolla 81, 82 below, 83, 86, 126 below; Colour Library Internat. 24, 115; Gerry Cranham 2–3, 119; Arthur Dailey 51 below; Findlay Davidson 95; Robert Estall 32; Mary Evans Picture Library 113 below; Fox Photos 60, 120 top, 122 below; William Hamilton (ZEFA) 50 below; Konrad Helbig (ZEFA) 61; Michael Holford 21, 56–57, 90 below; K. Jung (ZEFA) 27; Keystone Press Agency 26 below, 52 below, 116, 118 top; E. D. Lacey 93 top, 114 below, 120 below, 121 top, 122 top, 123, 125, 126 top; Colin Lofting 64 top l and r; James F. Logan 59; London Express News and Feature Services 114 top, 117; Jim Meads 118 below; Jane Miller l, 163, 165, 168 top; Morris Newcombe 82 top; Daniel O'Keefe 54 below, 87; Popperfoto 22; John Rigby 4, 128, 176; Peter Roberts 25, 53; W. Schmidt (ZEFA) 89; Spanish Riding School of Vienna 88, 90 top, 91, 92, 93 below, 96; Spectrum 23, 162, 164, 167, 169, 171, 174 top; Margie Spence 49 top, 51 top; Syndication Internat. 121 below, 124, 127; Sally Anne Thompson 26 top, 28–31, 49 below, 50 top, 52 top, 168 below, 172, 173, 174 below; Barbara Woolhouse 161; Adam Woolfitt 55; ZEFA 62, 63.

Index